CHILDREN AND YOUTH WITH

ASPERGER SYNDROME

CHILDREN AND YOUTH WITH
ASPERGER SYNDROME

BRENDA SMITH MYLES

STRATEGIES FOR SUCCESS IN INCLUSIVE SETTINGS

CORWIN PRESS
A SAGE Publications Company
Thousand Oaks, California

For information:

Corwin Press, Inc.
A Sage Publications Company
2455 Teller Road
Thousand Oaks California 91320
www.corwinpress.com

Sage Publications Ltd.
1 Oliver's Yard
55 City Road
London, EC1Y 1SP
United Kingdom

Sage Publications India Pvt. Ltd.
B-42, Panchsheel Enclave
Post Box 4109
New Delhi 110 017 India

Printed in the United States of America

Library of Congress Cataloging-in-Publication Data

Myles, Brenda Smith.
     Children and youth with Asperger syndrome: strategies for success in inclusive settings/ Brenda Smith Myles.
          p. cm.
Includes bibliographical references and index.
ISBN 1-4129-0497-8 (cloth) — ISBN 1-4129-0498-6 (pbk.)
     1. Asperger's syndrome—Patients—Education. 2. Autistic children—Education. 3. Autistic youth—Education. 4. Inclusive education. I. Title.
LC4717.5.M95 2005
371.94—dc22   2004028740

This book is printed on acid-free paper.

05   06   07   08   09   10   9   8   7   6   5   4   3   2   1

Acquisitions Editor:	Robb Clouse
Managing Editor:	Kylee Liegl
Editorial Assistant:	Jaime Cuvier
Production Editor:	Beth Bernstein
Copy Editor:	Diana Breti
Typesetter:	C&M Digitals (P) Ltd.
Proofreader:	Ruth Saavedra
Indexer:	Rick Hurd
Cover Designer:	Rose Storey

Contents

Foreword

T he complex, yet often subtle, needs of children and youth with
Asperger Syndrome often puzzle parents, professionals, and others
coming into contact with these individuals. Mostly exhibiting average to
above-average IQ and few, if any, distinctive physical characteristics, many
of these students are misunderstood and their behaviors misinterpreted.
Given that Asperger Syndrome has been included in the *Diagnostic and
Statistical Manual of Mental Disorders* only since 1994, only a few practical, user-friendly resources exist to turn to for help.

With *Children and Youth With Asperger Syndrome: Strategies for Success
in Inclusive Settings*, Brenda Smith Myles fills a yawning gap in the litera-
ture on autism spectrum disorders (ASD) for general educators. The book
discusses the characteristics of ASD and, more importantly, presents effective interventions for helping students with ASD and other pervasive
developmental disorders reach their greatest potential in the schools, ultimately permitting them to lead fulfilling and productive lives as contributing members of society.

Written to be immediately accessible to busy educators and others
coming in contact with students with Asperger Syndrome, the book starts
out with a comprehensive overview of the characteristics of ASD, with a
particular focus on the three major areas where ASD has an impact—
communication, social skills, and sensory issues. Assessment issues are
also addressed as necessary to designing appropriate programming.
Again, this is done in a straightforward "how to" manner based on the
author's extensive practical as well as theoretical and research knowledge
about individuals on the autism spectrum.

Each chapter opens with a short vignette or two fulfilling the dual purpose of bringing the content material alive for the reader and creating a
framework for addressing the myriad challenges school personnel face in

educating children with ASD, ranging from classroom accommodations to social interaction and emotional regulation. Examples sprinkled liberally throughout the book further sharpen the topics of discussion for the reader.

The hallmark of good educational planning and intervention for students with disabilities is when implementation of these techniques ends up benefiting the entire classroom of students, and thus serves as an extension of good teaching practice. In Chapter 3, examples of such interventions include the easy-to-remember mnemonics "Write Add Decide Execute" and "Sort Purge Assign Containerize Equalize," designed to help educators assist students with the difficult challenges of managing time and space, respectively, within their immediate surroundings. Chapter 4 is chock full of suggestions on providing the predictability and structure that is essential for the academic success of students with Asperger Syndrome. Many people who do not have Asperger Syndrome will most likely find these recommendations helpful as well.

In sum, *Children and Youth With Asperger Syndrome: Strategies for Success in Inclusive Settings* represents perfection in the art and science of combining research-based intervention and practical experiences with crystal-clear writing to set forth a cornucopia of practical, easy-to-implement interventions designed to provide students with Asperger Syndrome equal opportunity to excel in school with their peers. Where possible, the interventions are designed to de-emphasize students' differences from their classmates, thereby maximizing an inclusive atmosphere in the classroom.

As a person with Asperger Syndrome, it is clear to me and many of my peers that Brenda Smith Myles is one of the very rare persons who, in addition to understanding Asperger Syndrome, knows how to assist others to help those of us with this condition make sense of an often confusing educational environment and use our strengths to excel in school, and later on in life.

The outcome of Brenda's brilliant work is a book offering almost everything an educator needs to know to work effectively with children and youth with Asperger Syndrome.

—Stephen Shore
Doctoral candidate in special education, Boston University
Author of *Beyond the Wall: Personal Experiences
With Autism and Asperger Syndrome* and editor/coauthor of
Ask and Tell: Self-Advocacy and Disclosure for People on the Autism Spectrum

Acknowledgments

I would like to thank the following people who contributed to this project, either in the writing of, suggestions for, or critique of this book: Jill Hudson, Anastasia Hubbard, Spencer Nolan, Kristin Muellner, Kristen Hagen, Eileen Gorup, Jeanne Holverstott, Diane Adreon, Sean Smith, Nena Murphy-Herd, Daniel Alvarado, Nancy Glennon, Terri Cooper Swanson, Lindsay Hill, Sheila Smith, Ronda L. Schelvan, Lindsay Hall, Brandy Taylor, Alison Simonelli, Ginny L. Biddulph, and Kristen McBride. Their contributions were invaluable. Any errors in the book are my fault, not theirs.

Corwin Press gratefully acknowledges the contributions of the following reviewers:

Mary Jane Weiss, Director
Division of Research and Training
Rutgers University
New Brunswick, NJ

Arthur Arnold
Director of Special Education
Alaska State Department of
  Education
Juneau, AK

Gloria Wolpert
ASD Program Project Director
Manhattan College
Scarsdale, NY

Lisa S. Cushing, Professor
Department of Special Education
Vanderbilt University
Nashville, TN

Nicole Chiarello
Special Education Teacher
Bradford Elementary School
Cranston, RI

Monica Steward
Director of Special Education
Elizabethtown Area School District
Elizabethtown, PA

About the Author

Brenda Smith Myles, PhD is an associate professor in the Department of Special Education at the University of Kansas, where she co-directs a graduate program in Asperger Syndrome and autism. She has written numerous articles and books on Asperger Syndrome and autism, including *Asperger Syndrome and Difficult Moments: Practical Solutions for Tantrums, Rage, and Meltdowns* (with Southwick) and *Asperger Syndrome and Adolescence: Practical Solutions for School Success* (with Adreon), the winner of the Autism Society of America's Outstanding Literary Work Award. Myles is on the executive boards of several organizations, including Organization for Autism Research and Maap Services, Inc. She is also the editor of *Intervention in School and Clinic*, the second largest journal in special education.

About the Contributors

Diane Adreon, MA, is Associate Director of the University of Miami Center for Autism & Related Disabilities (UM-CARD). Ms. Adreon has presented nationally and internationally on Asperger's Disorder and has authored several articles on this subject. Ms. Adreon was an invited guest editor (with Myles) of a special issue on Assessment of Children and Youth with Autism Spectrum Disorders in *Assessment for Effective Intervention.* She serves as co-chair of the Professional Advisory Board of Maap Services Inc. (with Myles), as well as on the boards of Advocates for Individuals with HFA/AS/PDD, College Internship Program, and the ASA Chapter of Miami-Dade County. Ms. Adreon is co-author (with Myles) of *Asperger Syndrome and Adolescence: Practical Solutions for School Success* (2001 winner of the Autism Society of America Outstanding Literary Work Award). She is also on the editorial boards of Focus on Autism & Developmental Disorders and Intervention in School & Clinic.

Daniel Alvarado and Nancy Glennon are parents of a child with Asperger Syndrome. They have over 13 years of experience working with special educators, service providers, and clinicians in several communities across the country.

Terri Cooper Swanson, MS, coordinates research for the Autism & Asperger Syndrome program at the University of Kansas and is a consultant on Autism Spectrum Disorders. She received her masters of Special Education in Autism and Asperger Syndrome from the University of Kansas and is currently pursuing her doctoral degree. Terri has presented internationally and nationally and has written several articles and book chapters related to Autism Spectrum Disorders.

Anastasia Hubbard, MS, received her graduate degree in Asperger Syndrome and autism from the University of Kansas. She has worked internationally and nationally with individuals with Asperger Syndrome and autism, including serving as a consultant for home, school, and community-based programs. Ms. Hubbard works as a Project Coordinator for the University of Kansas' Interactive Collaborative Autism Network. She has authored several articles on Asperger Syndrome and autism for journals and newsletters. She is also the co-author of *Asperger Syndrome and Higher Education: Practical Solutions for a Successful University Experience.*

Jill Hudson, MS, received her graduate degree in Asperger Syndrome and autism from the University of Kansas. Ms. Hudson has served as a child life family specialist for children with Asperger Syndrome and other exceptionalities, as well as a camp counselor for children and youth with Asperger Syndrome and a social skills group coordinator. She is also the co-author of *Asperger Syndrome and Higher Education: Practical Solutions for a Successful University Experience.*

Mariangeles "Nena" Murphy-Herd, MS, is a doctoral student in special education with a minor in technology. Nena has worked in the area of assistive technology since 1982. She is a Field-Based Consultant for the Kansas State Department of Education and until returning to the university was the coordinator of the Educational Technology Service at The Capper Foundation.

Ronda L. Schelvan, MS, is currently on sabbatical from her teaching position with the Kelso, Washington School District. She has served as co-chairperson of Southwest Washington's Autism Consulting Cadre for the past four years. Ms. Schelvan has extensive experience working with students and families with special needs. She has presented at both local and state conferences and provided consulting services for families and school districts nationally.

Sean J. Smith, PhD, holds the rank of Assistant Professor of Special Education at the University of Kansas. Dr. Smith has a background in special education and technology, specifically towards the integration of technology across teacher preparation programs. He has authored and presented a number of articles and papers dealing with special education technology and is currently a Project Director on several Office of Special Education program initiatives seeking to further the integration of online technology components across teacher preparation programs and into the lives of students with disabilities.

Sheila M. Smith, MS, is a doctoral student at the University of Kansas. She has over 20 years of experience as a special educator. Prior to pursuing her doctoral studies, her most recent work experience included 10 years with Fairfax County Public Schools as a teacher of students with autism, an autism resource teacher, a special education administrator, and a staff developer.

Introduction

Characteristics of Children and Youth With Asperger Syndrome

CASE STUDY: BENNETT

Bennett, a six-year-old child with Asperger Syndrome, appears to have highly developed verbal skills since he is able to read aloud the daily newspaper with fluency, but he has difficulty asking and answering basic questions about his wants and needs. Often Bennett will show his frustration by crying or throwing himself to the floor when he is unable to express himself in a way that his teacher or peers understand. Changing activities can be stressful for Bennett, especially when the change is unexpected. Bennett will drop to the floor and whine instead of changing activities. During free play, he will position himself away from the other students, always choosing to use Lego's to build the Mars Land Rover, Space Shuttle, or Hubble Space Station.

CASE STUDY: OLIVIA

Olivia, a middle school student with Asperger Syndrome, began speaking at the same age as her peers, but she did not use speech fluently until the age of five. Although she has never been to England, her speech resembles that of someone from that country who speaks very formally and precisely. Academically she is at grade level or above, yet her social skills are limited. She lacks the skills to initiate, maintain, or terminate conversations. Her special interest of aerospace engineering borders on an obsession, which tends to discourage her peers from interacting with her because that is the subject she continually wants to talk about.

In the hallway between class periods, if someone asks Olivia, "Do you have the time?" (meaning "What time is it?") she interprets the question literally and responds by saying, "No, I am on my way to Mr. Desmond's class and I cannot be late!" or "Yes, I have the time. I have a new watch and it has a calculator, a stop watch, and an alarm." When Olivia becomes excited or nervous, she may rock forcefully in her chair or flick her fingers in front of her face. She will also refuse to participate in activities or experiences that involve close proximity to her peers, such as playing basketball in gym or working in groups on the floor. At other times, Olivia will "police" the hallway, pointing out rule infractions that students have committed and reminding students of the appropriate behaviors that should occur during passing times. Interactions such as these get Olivia labeled as being "really weird."

Developed by: Jeanne Holverstott

Despite the fact that Asperger Syndrome (AS) is an increasingly prevalent disability, it is not widely recognized. In fact, children and youth with AS are misunderstood partially because of the lack of information available about them, but also because of their inconsistent academic, emotional, and social behaviors. They have expressive language skills and intelligence quotients (IQ) that fall within the normal range, and yet they have social, emotional, and learning characteristics that make them a significant challenge for educators, parents, and the children themselves.

Generally, children and youth with AS receive the majority of their instruction in general education classrooms where teachers are expected to design and carry out their educational programs, including social skills training, often without training and frequently with little support from special educators. In recognition of these challenges, this book was written to familiarize general education classroom teachers and other personnel with the characteristics and educational strategies that have proven effective for this population of learners.

The disability now known as Asperger Syndrome was first discussed in 1944. However, this exceptionality was generally unknown in the United States until recently (Klin, Volkmar, & Sparrow, 2000; Myles & Simpson, 2003). The Identification and condition known as Asperger Syndrome is attributed to Hans Asperger, a Viennese physician who also studied a group of children who demonstrated a significant disability. Although Asperger observed that these children had many characteristics that were typical of children with autism, he stated that the children and youth he studied were different from those with autism.

For almost 40 years after Asperger's original work, virtually nothing related to AS was published. In 1981, however, a British psychiatrist, Lorna Wing, published a paper describing a group of individuals who presented with characteristics that seemed similar to those described by Hans Asperger. Awareness and recognition of Asperger Syndrome was further advanced in 1994 in the United States when the American Psychiatric Association added the syndrome to its list of pervasive developmental disorders, which it identified in its widely used *Diagnostic and Statistical Manual of Mental Disorders* (4th Edition) (American Psychiatric Association [APA], 1994).

Today the clinical term Asperger Syndrome is used by professionals, parents, and others throughout the world, including general education teachers who face the challenges associated with educating these children. There is still much we do not know about AS, including how many children have this disability (APA, 2000; Kadesjo, Gillberg, & Hagberg, 1999; Klin et al., 2000) and whether or not it is part of the autism spectrum or is an independent disability (Klin et al., 2000; Prior, 2003).

The attention on AS is, in part, related to its increased prevalence (Ehlers & Gillberg, 1993; Kadesjo et al., 1999) as well as the significant challenges that these students present for educators and families (Gill, 2003). Estimates on the number of students with AS are widely debated. For example, Volkmar and Klin (2000) reported "the present data are, at best, 'guesstimates' of its prevalence" (p. 62). Indeed, the most recent edition of the *Diagnostic and Statistical Manual of Mental Disorders* (DSM-IV, TR) (APA, 2000) omitted the prevalence estimate for AS because definitive data do not exist. Kadesjo et al. (1999), on the other hand, estimated that as many as 48 per 10,000 children may have AS. In the meantime, educators increasingly comment on the astonishing increase in the number of students diagnosed with AS, especially in general education programs.

Accompanying the increased recognition of AS is the awareness that much remains to be learned about this disorder. General education teachers and other educators who are responsible for planning for and teaching students with AS generally have not been provided the skills and knowledge to do so (Myles & Simpson, 2003). Crafting and implementing suitable supports and interventions for students with AS is especially difficult because of the lack of a clear understanding of the disorder, an absence of clearly defined educational methods and strategies, and scarce professional development programs. It is in this connection that this book was written. That is, strategies for educators are offered with special attention to general education teachers who teach children and youth diagnosed with AS. Strategies that can be used by special educators are also described in this book, so that all educational professionals have an awareness of the myriad supports that are needed to help children and youth with AS succeed in school.

IDENTIFICATION AND DIAGNOSIS OF CHILDREN AND YOUTH WITH ASPERGER SYNDROME

Clinically trained professionals, such as psychiatrists and clinical psychologists and other nonschool professionals, typically diagnose students with AS based on criteria provided in the DSM-IV, TR (APA, 2000). These criteria appear in Table I.1.

Even though school personnel do not directly rely on DSM-IV, TR criteria to make diagnoses of AS, they should be familiar with this widely used system. However, educators should keep in mind that the DSM-IV, TR does not provide a description of the characteristics of AS that most directly relate to school performance. Thus school professionals, especially general educators, must understand school-related social, behavioral/emotional, intellectual/cognitive, academic, sensory, and motor characteristics of students with AS.

Currently AS is a medical diagnosis that is often difficult to diagnose in the traditional medical setting. The characteristics of children and youth with AS are best seen (a) in interactions with peers, (b) in stressful situations, (c) in environments where the schedule or routine is not predictable, (d) when a high degree of structure is and is not in place, (e) when sensory stressors are apparent, and (f) in situations that are new for the students. These characteristics are evidenced over time in multiple environments and typically do not occur in a physician's office.

Since observations by physicians across multiple environments and over extended time is usually not feasible, the medical community must rely on the observations and reports of those who know the individual best—his or her teachers and parents—who have been shown to be reliable observers of children (Myles, Bock, & Simpson, 2000). Thus teachers and parents must be an essential part of the assessment process, including reporting behaviors that may lead medical practitioners to reliably identify AS. These factors must be communicated in a clear, consistent, and concise manner to physicians to ensure reliability and validity in diagnosis. The Asperger Syndrome Diagnostic Scale (ASDS) (Myles, Bock, et al., 2000), for example, was developed for this purpose. The ASDS is a norm-referenced instrument that parents and educators can complete and share with physicians to facilitate a diagnosis of children and youth.

Table I.1   DSM-IV TR Diagnostic Criteria for 299.80 Asperger's Disorder

❏ Qualitative impairment in social interaction, as manifested by at least two of the following:

- marked impairment in the use of multiple nonverbal behaviors such as eye-to-eye gaze, facial expression, body postures, and gestures to regulate social interaction
- failure to develop peer relationships appropriate to developmental level
- a lack of spontaneous seeking to share enjoyment, interests, or achievements with other people (e.g., by a lack of showing, bringing, or pointing out objects of interest to other people)
- lack of social or emotional reciprocity

❏ Restricted repetitive and stereotyped patterns of behavior, interests, and activities, as manifested by at least one of the following:

- encompassing preoccupation with one or more stereotyped and restricted patterns of interest that is abnormal either in intensity or focus
- apparently inflexible adherence to specific, nonfunctional routines or rituals
- stereotyped and repetitive motor mannerisms (e.g., hand or finger flapping or twisting, or complex whole-body movements)
- persistent preoccupation with parts of objects

❏ The disturbance causes clinically significant impairment in social, occupational, or other important areas of functioning.

❏ There is no clinically significant general delay in language (e.g., single words used by age 2 years, communicative phrases used by age 3 years).

❏ There is no clinically significant delay in cognitive development or in the development of age-appropriate self-help skills, adaptive behavior (other than in social interaction), and curiosity about the environment in childhood.

❏ Criteria are not met for another specific Pervasive Development Disorder or Schizophrenia.

SOURCE: APA, 2000.

SOCIAL AND COMMUNICATION CHARACTERISTICS

As originally noted by Asperger (1944), and confirmed by others (Frith, 1991; Myles & Adreon, 2001; Wing, 1981), the social and communication disorders within AS are particularly prominent. Children with AS are often socially isolated and demonstrate problems in interacting with others that cannot be explained by shyness, short attention span, aggression, or a lack of experience (Barnhill, 2001). However, individuals with AS want to interact with others despite their lack of skills. For example, an adolescent with AS may appear different from his peers because of his continuous insistence on sharing facts about washers and dryers, even though it is generally known by other students that nobody else is interested in this particular topic.

The social difficulties of persons with AS may range from social withdrawal and detachment to unskilled social activeness (Church, Alisanski, & Amanullah, 2000). Particularly challenging for both educators and peers is the fact that the social and communication challenges of children with AS may be masked by advanced verbal skills. That is, their one-sided conversational style and monologues on narrowly focused interests often lead others to believe that the child is socially competent. Those who know individuals with AS, however, recognize that they have communication and social problems. They often cannot share conversational topics and appear unwilling to listen to others. They are often perceived as adult-like, talking down to peers and teachers. The term "little professor" has been used to describe the speaking style of some children with AS (Myles & Simpson, 2003). Mali talks incessantly about Catherine the Great, not because she is rude but because she finds the topic extremely interesting. She does not understand why others do not share her passion. When children in her class begin to talk about the famous singer Beyonce's latest concert, Mali finds the topic of little importance and quickly tries to change the topic back to Catherine the Great.

Students with AS frequently have difficulty comprehending abstract concepts; understanding and correctly using metaphors, idioms, parables, and allegories; and grasping the meaning and intent of rhetorical questions. Because these conventions are commonly used in school settings, deficits in these areas negatively impact students' academic success. When Martin, a 10-year-old child with AS, was told by his teacher to "shake a leg," he began to do so—literally. He did not understand that he was supposed to hurry and became very upset when some of the children in class began to laugh at him.

Children and youth with AS often do not understand nonverbal cues—including facial expressions, gestures, voice tone, and physical proximity—that occur when interacting with others. In addition, they have difficulty understanding the thoughts, feelings, and perspectives of others, particularly when they differ from those of the individual with AS. To further add to the difficulty in understanding individuals, children and youth with AS may be able to infer the meaning of facial expressions as well as match events with facial expression in isolation; however, they are frequently unable to interpret or identify these variables when they occur simultaneously (Koning & McGill-Evans, 2001). This accounts for the inconsistent behavior of children who can name emotions when shown pictures or identify what they were to do in a social interaction, yet cannot use these skills in everyday life.

It is not unusual for students with AS to be able to engage in basic and introductory social interactions (e.g., basic greetings, asking someone her name) without being able to engage in reciprocal conversations. That is, many children and youth with AS are described by families and peers as (a) lacking awareness of social rules; (b) lacking common sense; (c) misinterpreting social prompts, cues, and unspoken messages; and (d) displaying a variety of socially unacceptable habits and behaviors (Gagnon & Myles, 1999). For example, Johanna told her parents that she played with her "best friends" at recess. It was not until her parents talked with Johanna's teacher that they understood what Johanna actually did at recess. Her teacher reported that Johanna would approach a small group of girls and say hello. She would then continue to stand near them and wait for a response, or she would immediately launch into a discussion of horse breeds. Even though her "best friends" would generally not respond, Johanna would just stand there. Not only were Johanna's parents at first unaware of their daughter's attempts at making friends at school, but Johanna's teacher had misinterpreted Johanna's behavior. She thought that Johanna just wanted to watch her peers and would interact appropriately with them when she was ready.

It is also common for students with AS to become easily stressed (Barnhill, 2001; Myles & Adreon, 2001). For example, students with AS may become upset if they think others are invading their space or when they are in unpredictable or novel social situations. However, in contrast to most of their peers, many children with AS do not reveal stress through voice tone, overt agitation, and so forth. As a result, they may escalate to a point of crisis because others are unaware of their excitement or discomfort, and because of their own inability to predict, control, and manage uncomfortable situations (Myles & Southwick, 1999). When John's teacher announced to the class that an assembly was scheduled in one hour, she noticed that John began to clear his throat rapidly. She knew that this seemingly minor behavior meant that John was stressed and might escalate to a tantrum. Therefore, she immediately went to him and talked with him about the assembly—who was featured, how long it would last, where John would sit, what John would do, and so on. She also wrote these things down as she spoke with John. Once John knew what was expected, he calmed himself and was able to attend the assembly with the rest of the class.

Although they lack social awareness, many students with AS are painfully aware that they are different from their peers. Thus self-esteem problems and self-concept difficulties are common. These problems are often particularly significant during adolescence and young adulthood (Myles & Adreon, 2001), when most individuals, including the most well-adjusted, are challenged in these areas.

The complexity of social situations and lack of rules that can be applied consistently make it difficult for students with AS to interact with others without instruction and support. Social rules vary, and their lack of consistency is confusing for children with AS. These individuals often painfully discover that interactions that may be tolerated or even reinforced in one setting are rejected or punished in others (Myles & Simpson, 2001). For example, one first-grade student with AS found it difficult to understand why his calling his teacher "Pee-Pee-Head" and "Mrs. Pee" in unsupervised settings such as the restroom was the source of great delight to his peers, while the same response in the classroom, in the presence of the teacher, Ms. Peters, drew a much different response.

Children and youth with AS do not automatically acquire greater social awareness as they get older. This is problematic in that students are required to use more sophisticated social skills and to interpret even more subtle social nuances as they progress through school. As a result, individuals with AS are vulnerable to developing a variety of problems. Studies of adolescents with AS have found out that they often experience discomfort and anxiety in social situations along with an inability to effectively interact with peers (Ghaziuddin, Weidmer-Mikhail, & Ghaziuddin, 1998). In addition, depression and anxiety may also occur (Barnhill, 2001; Ghaziuddin et al., 1998; Wing, 1981).

BEHAVIORAL AND EMOTIONAL CHARACTERISTICS

The behavioral and emotional problems experienced by children and youth with AS are often connected to their social deficits. Moreover, these problems and challenges frequently involve feelings of stress or loss of control or inability to predict outcomes (Myles & Southwick, 1999). In brief, students with AS typically have behavior problems connected to their inability to function in a world they see as unpredictable and threatening.

In one of the few studies that attempted to identify the nature of behavior problems and adaptive behavior among students with AS, Barnhill, Hagiwara, Myles, Simpson, Brick and Griswold (2000) compared the perceptions of parents, teachers, and students. The authors found that parents had significantly greater concern about the behavior and social skills of their children than did the students' teachers. Responses also revealed that parents perceived their children to have challenges in a variety of social and behavioral areas. Teachers, on the other hand, perceived the children and youth in the study to have both fewer and less significant deficits than did parents, although they did view the students to be "at risk" in the social and behavior areas. Students, on the other hand, reported that they were free of any social or behavioral challenges.

INTELLECTUAL AND COGNITIVE CHARACTERISTICS

A defining feature of AS is generally an average to above-average IQ (APA, 2000). However, given the importance of this variable, surprisingly little is known about the cognitive abilities of students diagnosed with AS.

In one of the few studies of the cognitive abilities of children and youth with AS, Barnhill, Hagiwara, Myles, and Simpson (2000) assessed the cognitive profiles of 37 children and youth with AS, as measured by the Wechsler scales (Wechsler, 1989, 1991). The scores generally fell within the average range of abilities, although the IQs ranged from intellectually deficient to very superior. It is important to note, however, that this and other studies have not identified a specific cognitive profile among individuals diagnosed with AS.

ACADEMIC CHARACTERISTICS

Because most students with AS receive their education primarily in general education classrooms, general education teachers are usually responsible for their education with the support of special educators and related services personnel.

In many ways, students with AS benefit from general classroom experiences. They typically have average to above-average IQs, are motivated to be with their general education peers, and often have good rote memory skills that support educational success. However, they often experience significant academic problems and many are thought also to have learning disabilities (Klin & Volkmar, 2000). In addition, students' special interests, concrete and literal thinking styles, inflexibility, and problem-solving and organizational challenges often make it difficult for them to benefit from general education placement without support and accommodations (Church et al., 2000). However, with support, many students with AS are able to be successful in school, and a number are able to attend college and enjoy successful careers.

Many teachers fail to recognize the special academic needs of children and adolescents with AS because these students often give the impression that they understand more than they do (Myles & Simpson, 2001). Their professor-like tone of voice, seemingly advanced vocabulary, rote-like responses, and ability to word recall without having comprehension skills to understand what they read may mask the deficits of some students with AS (Griswold, Barnhill, Myles, Hagiwara, & Simpson, 2002).

SENSORY CHARACTERISTICS

In his original study of children with AS, Asperger (1944) observed that his subjects had peculiar responses to sensory stimuli. Today this pattern continues, and teachers and parents often observe atypical sensory responses in the majority of children with AS they teach or live with (APA, 2000; Dunn, Myles, & Orr, 2002; Myles, Cook, Miller, Rinner, & Robbins, 2000). For example, it is not unusual for students with AS to be hypersensitive to certain visual stimuli, such as fluorescent lights, and particular sounds, such as the echoing noises common in a gym filled with playing children. Such sensitivity may cause anxiety and behavior problems.

Some individuals with AS have been reported to have an inconsistent tolerance for physical pain. Tijon tearfully begged his mother to take him to the hospital emergency room for his very painful hangnail. Tijon's mother could not believe that this was the same child who, last week, did not notice that he had a one-inch sliver of glass lodged in his foot.

Students with AS often engage in stereotyped or repetitive seemingly nonfunctional behaviors (e.g., obsessive object spinning, hand flapping), particularly when they are under stress, or when they experience fatigue, sensory overload, and so forth. The sensory issues seen in children and youth with AS appear similar to those of individuals with autism; however, their reactions to sensory issues seem more negative than those seen in individuals with autism. That is, students with AS are more likely to have a tantrum or other disruptive behaviors than children with autism when they have a sensory overload (Myles, Hagiwara, et al., 2004).

MOTOR CHARACTERISTICS

Wing (1981) and others have observed that children with AS often have poor motor skills along with coordination and balance problems (Dunn et al., 2002; Myles et al., 2000). These deficits are significant. First, being awkward and clumsy makes it difficult for students with AS to successfully participate in games requiring motor skills. Because participation in games and related activities is a social activity for children, problems in this area often go well beyond issues of motor coordination. Second, fine-motor skill difficulties may interfere with a variety of school activities, such as handwriting, art, and so forth (Myles et al., 2000).

SUMMARY

Children and youth with AS have many characteristics that place them at risk for school problems. Often misunderstood because of their average to above-average IQs and expressive language skills, these individuals have great potential that may go unrealized because of the modifications they require to be successful. The following chapters highlight myriad strategies that can be used to support students with AS in general education classroom settings.

Adaptations for Success in General Education Settings

1

with Jill Hudson

CASE STUDY: WILSON

Mrs. Blume announces, "Everyone, it is time to put your materials away and quietly line up for art class." The students follow the teacher's direction, closing their language arts books, putting their worksheets in their folders, placing the books and folders in their desks, pushing their chairs in and then quietly lining up at the door. Mrs. Blume, noticing that Wilson is still sitting at his desk reading his language arts book, asks, "Wilson, why have you not put all of your materials away and gotten in line like the rest of the children? You need to listen." Wilson, not understanding why he is being scolded, shows his frustration by crying and throwing himself to the floor.

CASE STUDY: TALIA

The bell rings. Children rush through the hallway toward their lockers, to the restroom, to say hello to a friend. Quickly they shuffle along and return in a few minutes to the classroom, settling back into their seats and pulling out their work. With the teacher's instruction, they quiet down and begin working. Talia comes stumbling through the door, dragging her backpack full of books behind her. As she makes her way to her seat, she bumps a couple of desks and says, "Hey, what are you guys doing? Did you see the guy in the hallway?" The teacher interrupts and redirects Talia to her seat. Talia nevertheless continues with her story, giving dramatic details and tripping over others as she makes her way to her seat. Once seated, she fumbles through her bag, pulling out her book with papers crammed inside. She blurts out loudly to her teacher, "Do you have a pencil?" Mrs. Smith closes her eyes and thinks to herself, "What am I supposed to do?"

Developed by: Jeanne Holverstott

These scenarios are all too familiar to many teachers. Children coming in late, not prepared with materials or work for the day, and interrupting with details irrelevant to class. With class size increasing and the needs of students continually diversifying, the typical classroom is often a challenge to manage.

Within each classroom, a certain level of expectation must be met in order for the class to run efficiently and effectively. However, expectations vary from teacher to teacher and across settings. Knowledge of expectations is critical for students to succeed in a particular classroom. Thus, their ability to predict, understand, and perform to the level required reflects on their achievement as well as their ability to advance. Nevertheless, while each teacher's expectations vary, certain expectations that support a well-run classroom are consistent across grade levels. Expectations and other tools that are effective in the classroom are discussed in this chapter.

BEHAVIOR EXPECTATIONS

Studies conducted across all grade levels show that teachers consistently look for and expect similar classroom behaviors in spite of the grade level taught (Hersh & Walker, 1983; Kerr & Zigmond, 1986; Lane, Pierson, & Givner, 2003; Walker & Rankin, 1983). In addition, when they list undesirable or intolerable behaviors within the classroom setting, they are closely related as well. As shown in Table 1.1, the findings of research into teacher expectations suggest that teachers rate behaviors such as self-control, cooperation, overall discipline, and ability to follow teacher direction as most critical and more important than social interactions with peers and related behaviors.

While teachers agree overall on the behaviors that promote a positive learning environment, some differ depending on grade level. That is, elementary and high school teachers tend to value some behaviors differently (Hersh & Walker, 1983; Kerr & Zigmond, 1986; Lane et al., 2003; Walker & Rankin, 1983). For example, as shown in Table 1.1, overall, elementary-grade teachers place less value on items that relate to peer-to-peer relationships, such as initiating conversation with peers, while stressing the importance of behaviors that directly impact *their* interaction with students, such as following written and oral directions. Elementary-grade teachers generally consider half as many behaviors critical for the classroom as high school teachers, though they rank many as desirable. Table 1.2 compares the top 10 behaviors rated critical for classroom success by high school teachers with the top 10 of those teaching elementary grades. Though there are many similarities between the two lists, the degree to which behaviors are valued varies.

Table 1.1 Overview of Research on Student Behaviors in General Education Classrooms

Author/Year	Number of Participants	Grade Level	Method	Survey	Data Collection System	Results
Lane, Pierson, and Givner (2003)	366 general and special education teachers	K–12	Teachers ranked 30 items according to how important they were to school success	Social Skills Rating Scale by Gresham and Elliot, 1990	0 = not important 1 = important 3 = critical	Five skills were critical: follow directions, attend to instruction, control temper in peer conflict, control conflicts with adults, and respond appropriately to peer physical aggression
Kerr and Zigmond (1986)	244 total general and special education teachers	9–12	Teachers evaluated 107 items in two subgroups: appropriate behaviors and inappropriate behaviors	SBS Inventory of Teacher Social Behavior Standards and Expectations by Walker and Rankin, 1980	Appropriate behavior scale 1 = unimportant 2 = desirable 3 = critical Inappropriate behavior scale 1 = acceptable 2 = tolerated 3 = unacceptable	26 appropriate behavior items were ranked as critical by 50% of teachers; 14 inappropriate behavior items were ranked as unacceptable by 90% of teachers
Walker and Rankin (1983)	50 general education and 22 special education	1–6	Teachers were asked to evaluate 107 items in two subgroups: appropriate behaviors and inappropriate behaviors	SBS Inventory of Teacher Social Behavior Standards and Expectations by Walker and Rankin, 1980	Appropriate behavior scale 1 = unimportant 2 = desirable 3 = critical Inappropriate behavior scale 1 = acceptable 2 = tolerated 3 = unacceptable	Over 50% of maladaptive items received an "unacceptable" rating. Items of least significance to teachers were social interactions with peers. Adaptive items ranked highly most often included classroom control, general discipline, and compliance with teacher directions. Maladaptive items ranked highly most often included high intensity/low incidence (e.g. stealing, self-abuse, teacher defiance).

Table 1.2   Teachers' Perceptions of Essential Student Behaviors

High School

1. Follows established classroom rules
2. Attends to and follows oral instructions given for assignments
3. Attends to and follows written teacher instruction
4. Complies with teacher commands
5. Completes assignments in class when required
6. Responds appropriately to peer pressure pertaining to following classroom rules
7. Produces work corresponding with ability and skill level
8. Possesses effective classroom management skills—efficient, organized, on-task
9. Requests assistance in an appropriate manner when needed
10. Copes with failure in an appropriate manner

Elementary School

1. Complies with teacher commands
2. Follows established classroom rules
3. Produces work corresponding with ability and skill level
4. Attends to and follows oral instructions given for assignments
5. Expresses anger appropriately
6. Interacts with peers without becoming hostile or angry
7. Regulates behavior in non-classroom settings
8. Responds appropriately to peer pressure pertaining to following classroom rules
9. Completes assignments in class when required
10. Requests assistance in an appropriate manner when needed

A comparison of teacher tolerance across grade levels is also interesting. When provided a list of inappropriate behaviors, elementary-grade teachers ranked over half of the maladaptive behaviors as "unacceptable." In comparison, only 14 behaviors were rated "unacceptable" by at least 90% of the high school teachers. So while the high school teachers demand more, the elementary-grade teachers tolerate less. Table 1.3 compares the maladaptive behaviors most often rated "unacceptable" by high school teachers and by elementary teachers.

While understanding behavioral characteristics is important, one must also realize that the image each student projects impacts how teachers and others perceive them and interact with them. Richard Lavoie (cited in Bieber, 1994) has outlined several characteristics that should be taught to all students in every classroom because they are held in high esteem by adults and student peers.

1. Smiling and laughing. All children enjoy seeing another child smile. It is contagious and keeps the atmosphere of the room light and positive.

2. Greeting others. Teach the students to say hello to others as they pass in the hallway. It is friendly and encourages students to keep their heads up as they change classes.

Table 1.3   Teachers' Perceptions of Inappropriate Classroom Behaviors

High School

1. Engages in inappropriate sexual behavior
2. Steals
3. Is physically aggressive against others
4. Behaves inappropriately in class when corrected
5. Damages others' property
6. Refuses to obey teacher-imposed classroom rules
7. Disturbs or disrupts the activities of others
8. Is self-abusive
9. Makes lewd or obscene gestures
10. Ignores teacher warnings or reprimands

Elementary School

1. Steals
2. Is self-abusive
3. Retaliates in class when corrected
4. Is physically aggressive with others
5. Makes lewd or obscene gestures
6. Engages in inappropriate sexual behavior
7. Refuses to obey teacher-imposed classroom rules
8. Damages others' property
9. Throws tantrums
10. Ignores teacher warnings and reprimands

3. Extending invitations. When students are going out together or starting an activity, encourage them to include others and to always look for additional participants.

4. Conversing. Communication skills are important to express, request, and comment on a variety of scenarios throughout the day. Help students understand the basic rules of communication, how to initiate a conversation and take turns, and how to take interest in others.

5. Sharing. No one enjoys a student who keeps everything to himself. Encourage students to work together and collaborate on projects and share supplies.

6. Giving compliments. Everyone enjoys knowing what is special about him or her. Make a point to express when a student does something well or when he or she is appreciated.

7. Good appearance. Hygiene and grooming are important for self-esteem, cleanliness, and positive interactions among peers.

Lavoie has also outlined a list of behaviors that will help students be successful. He calls this list the "No Sweats," as they take relatively little time to learn as well as minimal effort and energy to do.

1. Be on time.

2. Establish eye contact when speaking or listening.

3. Participate, either by giving input to a discussion or simply by asking a question.

4. Use the teacher's name.

5. Submit work on time.

6. Use the required format for assignments and projects.

7. Avoid crossing out on papers.

8. Request explanations instead of giving up when not understanding.

9. Thank the teacher for his or her effort and time.

If these skills and behaviors are taught in the classroom and included as expectations, a general education classroom can be expected to run more harmoniously.

CONSISTENCY AND CLEAR COMMUNICATION OF EXPECTATIONS

Communication of expectations is the key (Backes & Ellis, 2003). Often students "misbehave" because they do not clearly understand what is expected. Three to five classroom rules may be posted that contain items such as "Be courteous." Without a specific definition of what that rule entails, it is left open to a variety of interpretations and may be widened or narrowed according to each child's personal analysis. In addition to general classroom behavior, expectations are assumed for personal conduct, safety, and assignments and should be clearly outlined or stated to ensure understanding. Since many students move through several teachers and classrooms in a given day, it is helpful to define, set, and uphold expectations in a similar manner.

Members of the same profession do not always agree on expected outcomes. Therefore, those who interact with the child need to determine what is desired by all team members so that when individual members teach students about appropriate behaviors, the students are meeting the larger set of expectations across all settings.

EXPECTATIONS IN PRACTICE

Teacher expectations must be translated into rules and routines that students understand. Most students without disabilities are able to infer these expectations. However, for many students with disabilities, teacher expectations remain a mystery. General education expectations can be operationalized into four groups: (a) response to teacher, (b) interactions with peers, (c) self-regulation, and (d) classroom performance. These expectations are not always easy to follow or understand when they are not explicitly written out or taught. Often rules are posted, but expectations are inferred and vary from task to task. Therefore, to maintain and perform at a level consistent with the general expectations that fall into these four categories, students must use combined components from social, communication, and cognitive domains. For some children, performing to desired expectations poses a genuine challenge. Having to pay attention to only one component at a time prevents them from being able to multitask and perform consistently at the level expected without supports from the school environment. Students with Asperger Syndrome (AS) fall into this category.

Response to Teacher

Response to the teacher is defined as those behaviors that directly relate to the instructor. Listening to teacher instructions, complying with requests, asking questions, and seeking help appropriately fall into this category.

Listening to Teacher Instructions and Complying With Requests

Students with AS generally process directions and instructions better when given in a concrete, visual manner. Therefore, when instructions are given only verbally they are often not able to accurately process and follow them. In the first case study above, Wilson is unable to process Mrs. Blume's verbal directions. Mrs. Blume, not understanding that Wilson has difficulty processing verbal instructions, thinks he is misbehaving and scolds him. Wilson does not understand why he is being scolded because he had not heard the instructions. He begins to cry and falls to the floor. However, when Wilson was unable to get started on his math assignment, Mrs. Smith wrote the directions on the paper in three steps in addition to verbally stating it. After receiving written instruction, Wilson was able to complete the assignment with little additional assistance.

Asking Questions and Seeking Help Appropriately

When a student with AS needs a pencil, other class supply, or assistance, he may blurt out the request without paying attention to the context of the situation—that is, that students are to raise their hands to get the teacher's attention. In the second case study, Talia has disrupted class and she blurts loudly that she needs a pencil instead of quietly raising her hand until the teacher calls on her. By learning a method through which to make the request (i.e., raising her hand), the student has an outlet to receive what she needs in a manner that complies with the environment.

Interaction With Peers

Interaction with peers consists of behaviors such as conversing with and relating to peers and collaborating with peers.

Conversing With and Relating to Peers

Communication and interaction with peers can be a great challenge to students with AS because they often lack skills to detect facial cues and other nonverbal cues and fail to understand social subtleties. In addition, depending on their special interests as well as developmental level, students with AS may or may not relate to their same-age peers. Thus, some students may need instruction and support in learning how to join a group of children and suggestions for how to maintain interactions.

Collaborating With Peers

Children with AS have many ideas and thoughts and are often driven to follow through with them. This is both an asset and a deterrent to working in groups. These students, when motivated by a topic of interest, are diligent workers carrying out their idea to completion. However, when in a group situation, if challenged on their ideas, they become frustrated and overwhelmed and, as a result, may act out or have a tantrum, rage, or meltdown. With written and oral instructions and clear role guidelines for group participation, the student with AS knows what is expected and can be a better group member. Jimmy was on a team with four other boys for a state problem-solving competition. Round one was a brainstorm session of ideas that could possibly solve the given problem. Round two consisted of choosing one team member's idea and expanding it into an elaborative plan to solve the problem. In practice, Jimmy was continually frustrated when the other boys did not select his idea. He would get mad and stop participating in the group for the remainder of the competition. When the structure of the process was drawn out on paper—showing the brainstorming and elimination of ideas as well as explaining the role Jimmy would continue to play as the team moved into round two—he was better able to anticipate, predict the situation, and therefore prepare himself to transition from round one to round two and be an active participant.

Self-Regulation

Self-regulation includes behaviors the child will monitor himself, such as finishing assigned work appropriately, coping with successes and failures, overseeing and controlling personal behavior, and actively participating in class.

Finishing Assigned Work Appropriately

Understanding what criteria a particular teacher uses when grading assignments is helpful for the student with AS. When students with AS are given projects or assignments without specific instruction, they easily become overwhelmed, which can lead to a tantrum, rage, or meltdown. Without knowing how to manage the load, they may become negative about getting started or question the worth of completing a given project. Assisting the child to develop a plan of organization and break the project into many smaller, more manageable tasks helps the child know what to do and prevents anxiety. In addition, this type of activity helps create an outlying structure for time management so the student does not leave all the details to the last minute.

The science fair was only two weeks away and Marcus was overwhelmed by the amount of work he had left to do. He felt as if there were so many expectations that he could not accomplish any of them. Since he felt he was failing to make progress, he no longer wanted to attempt any tasks. He did not think the project was worth his time because he could not complete all of the requirements in the designated time. He shut down, became obstinate, and refused to work. After Marcus had a chance to calm down, Mrs. Tatum talked with him about how to approach each task. They made a timeline that incorporated all of the tasks that needed to be accomplished. Mrs. Tatum helped Marcus focus on one task at a time, setting short-term, manageable goals. Marcus was able to pace himself and work again when he was presented with just one small piece of the project at a time.

Coping With Changing Emotions of Success and Failure

The emotional status of children with AS can be volatile. Reinforcement of desired behavior is recommended instead of punishing undesirable behaviors. This allows the child to concretely understand what is expected of her or him. It is important, however, to reinforce in a timely manner and directly and concretely relate the desired action to the reinforcer. Because Savannah becomes easily overwhelmed by math, Mr. Williams regulates and rewards her behavior by using a management system in which Savannah is involved and that she understands. When Savannah completes the allotted number of math problems, she takes a break and plays on the computer for five minutes. After the five minutes, Savannah returns to her desk to complete her next work task.

When emotions change quickly, such as when a student with AS becomes overwhelmed, it is beneficial for the child to take a break to calm himself before instruction or redirection is given.

Overseeing and Regulating Own Behavior

Students with AS need to know what behavior options are available to them. Many students with AS do not realize that alternatives to becoming overly frustrated exist. When Suzanna came into her third-period class, she quietly let her teacher know that she needed to go to her home base and cool down after being inadvertently pushed and touched many times in the hallway on the way to class. Instead of retaliating against the offending students, Suzanna utilized a predetermined plan that she had been taught by her teacher, which gave her an opportunity to make a good choice as well as regulate her behavior. Just as she had been taught, she gripped the handles of her backpack tighter and walked straight to her teacher. Once she had permission to go to her home base, Suzanna was able to find her putty and pull on it to help her calm herself. Once she felt calm, she was able to return to her seat in the classroom and participate in the assignment.

Actively Participating

In order to actively participate in class, most students with AS need adequate time to process the situation, comment, or question. Developing a signal to give the child as a warning that you will ask a question will allow her to prepare an answer. For example, stating the question, pausing, and then asking for the answer allows the child time to process the question as well as formulate an answer. Often the child is still processing the first question when the class has answered it and a second question is asked. Mrs. Jones asked, "What is the capital of Texas?" Jose, in his mind, goes through these steps: "What . . . means asking a question. Capital is a specific city . . . Texas is the state she mentioned. What is the capital of Texas? Oh, it is Austin." Jose enthusiastically raised his hand and said

"Austin," unaware that Leah had already answered and Mrs. Jones had moved on and was now asking for the capital of Idaho.

Following the above suggestions, Mr. Lui stepped in front of Shanequa's desk, asked, "What are the three branches of the American government?" and then turned and erased the overhead, giving time for the students to think. Shanequa recognized Mr. Lui's signal of coming near her desk and asking a question. Carefully she thinks over what he asked. In her mind she reviews, "What are the three branches of the American government? . . . American government . . . branches . . . three of them . . . I know this." Shanequa looks up at Mr. Lui once she has determined her answer. He finishes erasing the overhead and sees her signal back that she has processed and is ready. Calling on her first, Mr. Lui states her name and then requests the information again. "Shanequa, can you name one branch of the American government?" Confidently, Shanequa gives the correct answer.

Classroom Performance

Appropriate performance in the classroom setting entails those behaviors that affect overall classroom conduct, such as utilizing materials and resources in the classroom and working independently.

Following Established Rules

Children with AS have a great affinity for rule following. When a routine or procedure is clearly defined and taught, the student with AS can often perform within guidelines and will hold other children accountable to the expectation as well. However, when a rule is stated and not explained, the student with AS may violate it because of a lack of understanding. In addition, if a general educator teaches a rule but does not apply or reinforce it consistently, the child with AS may attempt to enforce it himself. While the child perceives this action as "helping the teacher," everyone else will likely see it differently. John, a 10-year old with AS, grabbed the pencil Mike was tapping on his desk and broke it because Mike did not stop tapping at the teacher's request. John did not understand why he incurred consequences for invading Mike's personal space and destroying his pencil, thinking that he was simply enforcing the rule that was clearly stated by the teacher.

Utilizing Academic Tools and Resources

Items that are commonplace in a classroom are not always so obvious to a student with AS. How and when to use a dictionary, table of contents, or index, for example, can be confusing and overwhelming. Instruction may need to be given in detail to introduce a child to the various resources in the classroom and assistance given to make the best choice of resources to use with a particular assignment.

Working Independently

If a student with AS is having a calm day, is caught up with his assignments, and feels comfortable with a task, he is often able to attend to and complete a task. However, if the student is in a heightened state of anxiety, feels he has too much to do, or becomes overwhelmed by the task, he may blurt out or have a meltdown. The clarity of instructions given and the student's level of understanding will set the pace for getting started on schoolwork. The child may sit staring at the work, overwhelmed, not knowing what to do. It is commonplace for a student with AS to be able to quote back directions that were verbally given without actually comprehending the meaning of the words, and therefore, not knowing how to follow those directions. The teacher can assist the student by allowing time and space for the child to settle down if agitated. Also, demonstrating the first item or working through the beginning of an assignment with the child allows him to better understand what to do.

Organizing Materials

Often organization is a challenge for the student with AS. A student may finish her homework, albeit more slowly than others, but getting it into her backpack, to school, and eventually to the teacher is where the problem lies. Using a notebook with dividers, color-coding books and materials for each class, or giving pictures of what is needed for a specific event or situation assists the child by giving structure and concrete support.

Transitioning Across Settings

Because of the varied expectations across teachers and settings, transition between class subjects or between classrooms can prove difficult for some students with AS. Even within the classroom, transitioning from one task to another can be difficult when the child has not completed the original task given. If it is necessary for the child to move on, the teacher may simply draw a finished line (a heavy line drawn using a marker) under the last task completed or break down a large project into several smaller ones. This allows the student to see where the assignment ends and get a sense of completion that will allow her to move on to the next task. Priming, that is, giving enough information about an upcoming change or task before it occurs, allows the child to prepare for the shift in the environment and his or her schedule.

Understanding Concepts

Although they have an average to above-average intelligence level and baseline knowledge in a particular academic area, students with AS do not always understand abstractions. Using concrete examples, visuals, and manipulatives to assist students in experiencing a concept gives them an opportunity to better understand.

SUMMARY

General educators place many demands on their students. Often these demands involve unspoken rules and expectations whose violation may have serious repercussions, such as not being able to complete assignments, being shunned by peers, and experiencing anxiety related to a lack of clarity in class structure and assignments. Children must be taught the behaviors expected in classrooms beginning in elementary school and continuing through high school. For example, elementary students with AS will greatly benefit from instruction in behaviors that allow teachers to conduct a smoothly run class. In addition, instruction in LaVoie's "No Sweats" provides the student with the means to interact with teachers in a positive manner. When these otherwise elusive social and behavioral mores are directly taught, the student with AS is more likely to be successful in the general education classroom setting.

Environmental Modifications

2

with Anastasia Hubbard

CASE STUDY: MOLLY

Molly is a seventh grader in an inclusive setting at a middle school. When her teacher, Mrs. Moore, first met Molly, she described her as a polite, though rather shy, student whose intelligence was evident in the way she spoke about space shuttles. Molly reminded her of some students she had worked with previously and even of a few students who would also be in Molly's class. As Mrs. Moore interacted with Molly in their classroom throughout the following weeks, though, she noticed some characteristics that she had not noticed, at least not to the same extent, in other students with whom she had worked. Molly spoke in a rather adult-like manner, yet she often did not seem to listen to and follow even the simplest of directions. Molly also expressed anxiety about what would occur during class, sometimes asking Mrs. Moore as many as five times in a 45-minute period what they were going to do next, but seeming never to remember the answers to this question. Despite Molly's politeness, Mrs. Moore often felt she was being noncompliant. For example, when the bell rang at the end of the class period, Molly often continued to work at her desk and did not comply with Mrs. Moore's requests to pack up her belongings and move on to her next class. As Mrs. Moore noticed more and more of these characteristics in Molly, she became increasingly frustrated. She tried talking with her and sharing ideas with her for how she could improve, but that did not seem to help. It was not until she decided to work with the special education coordinator to learn more about Molly's diagnosis of AS that the meaning of her behaviors became clearer and she was able to help Molly succeed in her classroom.

Developed by: Jeanne Holverstott

Students with AS may not look much different from other students. However, as previously discussed, these students have a variety of characteristics that may challenge educators to think about how to interact with them and how to help them learn in an entirely new way. Every student learns differently

15

and requires different modifications. Unlike many of their neurotypical peers, students with AS are often unable to recognize and monitor their own strengths and challenges and subsequently make or ask for modifications. This is an important challenge to which educators need to be attentive.

One of the reasons Mrs. Moore was able to help Molly was that she tried to view all aspects of the school environment from Molly's perspective. As described in Chapter 1, individuals with AS often have difficulties understanding the perspective of another person. For Molly, this meant that she was often unable to understand or infer what she should or should not be doing, what Mrs. Moore expected of her students, and so forth. Mrs. Moore found ways to address these challenges and help Molly improve by considering how Molly viewed the school environment. For example, to her and many of her students, a ringing bell signaled a typical transition—time for students to stop what they are doing, pack up their supplies, and move on to their next class. Molly's perspective differed. To her, a ringing bell meant, "Oh no! The bell rang. Wait! I haven't packed up my supplies yet. And I am still finishing this math problem. I have to finish this math problem before I can go to music."

Through observations and informal interviews with Molly, some of her other teachers, and her dad, Mrs. Moore learned that she was not the only one who noticed Molly's difficulty with transitions. An informal conversation with Molly proved particularly helpful in understanding her perspective. Mrs. Moore asked her why she felt she had to finish a math problem that she was in the middle of when the bell rang, rather than stop and take it home to finish. Molly answered, "Because you told me that we had five problems to complete before leaving class today." That simple sentence gave Mrs. Moore a great deal of insight into Molly's perspective on the situation. While Molly's classmates instantly problem-solved when the bell rang by deciding to take home any math problems they had not finished in class, Molly recalled the specific instruction that Mrs. Moore gave the students—to complete five math problems before leaving class. She felt she needed to follow through with this exactly as stated by Mrs. Moore. She did not believe she was being noncompliant when she did not follow Mrs. Moore's instructions to pack up her belongings and move on to her next class. Rather, she felt she was being compliant and just following through with the original instruction that Mrs. Moore gave her.

This chapter outlines the types of information educators should gather about their students with AS and presents specific environmental modifications based on this information that can be implemented to help these students succeed. As Molly and Mrs. Moore's story indicates, and as will be described further in this chapter, some of the most important supports that teachers can offer students with AS are individualization, understanding, structure, predictability, consistency, flexibility, and patience. These address characteristics that many students with AS may have, as discussed in Chapter 1.

LEARNING ABOUT THE STUDENT WITH AS

While it is important to understand the general characteristics and needs of individuals with AS, it is critical to understand the unique characteristics and needs of specific students with AS, as no two students with AS are alike. Observations and interviews are two ways to accomplish this. Information should be gathered on the student's strengths, challenges, interests, goals, and learning style. A list of questions that can be presented to the student, and a list of questions that can be presented to school team members, service providers, and parents are provided below.

Questions for Students

1. What do you like about school?

2. What do you like about your school day?

3. What do you not like about school?

4. What do you not like about your school day?

5. What helps you learn?

6. What helps you have a good day at school?

7. If you could learn about anything you wanted, what would it be?

8. What are your goals for yourself when you come to school each day?

Questions for Teachers, Additional Service Providers, and Parents

1. What are the student's strengths?

2. What are the student's challenges?

3. What are your goals for this student?

4. What does the student like to learn about?

5. What does the student not like to learn about?

6. What conditions have you observed that have helped him or her learn?

7. What modifications or strategies have you tried with the student that have worked well?

8. What modifications or strategies have you tried that have not worked well?

To best utilize information collected in this manner, the Snapshot of Learner Characteristics, shown in Figure 2.1, provides a concise format for recording information about the student with AS relevant to a particular area or task. It includes sections to describe the area or task and the related goals and objectives for the student. Additionally, it includes sections for information on how the student learns best (including sensory needs), what environmental and academic adaptations the student may benefit from, including motivators, organizational strategies, assessment-related information, and social skills. It also informs the reader whether the snapshot has been completed based on student, teacher, or parent input.

School teams may use Snapshots in a variety of ways. One student's school team may want to create a Snapshot for each of the major developmental domains such as communication skills, motor skills, self-help skills, academic skills, and so forth. Another student's school team may choose to complete a Snapshot for each of the student's class periods, such as English, social studies, science, and physical education. No formula exists for how Snapshots are best used; what is most important is that Snapshots *are* used. They are documents that provide a great deal of insight regarding the student in a concise, easy-to-read format. They should not only be referred to on a daily basis, but should also be included in a student's "personal files," as discussed in Chapter 8. Figure 2.2 is a sample Snapshot for Maria that focuses on her seventh-grade science class.

EMPOWERING THE STUDENT WITH AS

A crucial aspect of helping the individual with AS reach her full potential is to involve her in the process of collecting information, deciding which supports and modifications may best assist her, and engaging her in developing materials associated with these supports and modifications. While it may seem as though it would be easier and faster to assess the student's needs and decide on one's own what might best help her, it is imperative to allow the student with AS to be a part of this process:

- Seek her input about her strengths, challenges, interests, goals, and learning style
- Involve her in developing modifications, strategies, etc., including the creation of any materials that will be used to accompany these

(Text continues on page 21)

Figure 2.1   Snapshot of Learner Characteristics

STUDENT NAME: _____

> **Area or Task:** (for instance: social skills, communication skills, motor skills, English, science, reading, math, etc.)
>
> **Goals/Objectives:**

> **Learns Best:** (please consider sensory needs as a component of this)

> **Environmental and Curriculum-Based Modifications and/or Supports:**

> **Motivators:**

> **Organizational Strategies:**

> **Assessment Modifications and/or Strategies:**

> **Social Skills:**

Input Received From: **Other:**

    Student   _____

    Teacher(s)   _____

    Parent(s)   _____

Figure 2.2   Sample Snapshot of Learner Characteristics

STUDENT NAME: _____ Maria T. _____

Area or Task: (for instance: social skills, communication skills, motor skills, English, science, reading, math, etc.)

Science

Goals/Objectives:

- Maria will strive to learn the content of her 7th-grade science class with opportunities to demonstrate her knowledge of it through means that match her strengths and challenges.
- Maria will attend her 7th-grade science class 80% of the time. If she chooses not to attend class, she will complete a comparable assignment in her resource room.

Learns Best: (please consider sensory needs as a component of this)

- Visually
- When sitting in front row in classroom
- When provided with concrete examples and/or hands-on learning opportunities
- When able to predict what will come next
- When able to use a fidget item as necessary

Environmental and Curriculum-Based Modifications and/or Supports:

- Visual supports: especially in the form of task schedules, lists, and graphic organizers
- Ensure Maria has at least 24" between her desk and any other person's desk
- Priming: preview class information and/or activities prior to class period
- Modified assignments: minimal amount of handwriting required, or may complete orally or use computer, scribe, or tape recorder; highlight important information
- Limit homework to 15 minutes per night for this subject

Motivators:

- *Anything related to horses*
- *The Princess Diaries books*
- *Potato chips, popcorn, cola*

Organizational Strategies:

- Daily planner/assignment notebook with map of school on inside front cover
- Lists
- Daily schedule

Assessment Modifications and/or Strategies: Use alternate forms of assessment; minimize writing required; may take verbally; may use scribe or tape recorder; allow extended time to complete

Social Skills:

- Strengths: will respond to others when they initiate interactions
- Challenges: conversation—initiating, reciprocating, maintaining

---

Input Received From:

Student	X
Teacher(s)	X
Parent(s)	X

Other:

- Make learning meaningful to her through such means as incorporating her interests into the curriculum
- Build from her strengths
- Provide positive reinforcement

Once the educator has collected information about the student and empowered her to be a part of this process, she and the student can work as a team to implement modifications, including environmental changes.

THE SCHOOL ENVIRONMENT

Classroom Layout

All students benefit from a well-organized classroom. Components of such a classroom include:

1. Clearly defined areas for each activity

2. Visual reminders of classroom expectations

3. Adequate spacing to allow for personal space preferences, such as sitting at least 24" from another person

4. Organization of materials, for example, by color coding and labeling (with written words, pictures, or both)

A well-organized environment often proves particularly beneficial for students with AS as it provides the structure, predictability, and visual supports that many of them need. It informs them where to be, where to obtain items, where to return items, and what the classroom expectations are. Figure 2.3 is an example of what a well-organized classroom may look like.

Home Base

Students with AS may benefit from having a home base—a quiet place in the school where they can go to (a) plan or review information or (b) cope with stress and behavioral challenges (Myles & Adreon, 2001; Myles & Southwick, 1999). There are no specific criteria for the location of a home base—it may be located anywhere that is comforting to the student, such as a resource room, a favorite teacher's classroom, or a staff member's office. The student may want to spend time at home base in the morning to review his schedule for the day and the activities that lie ahead. Home base also serves as a place the student can go if the classroom

Figure 2.3   Sample Organized Classroom

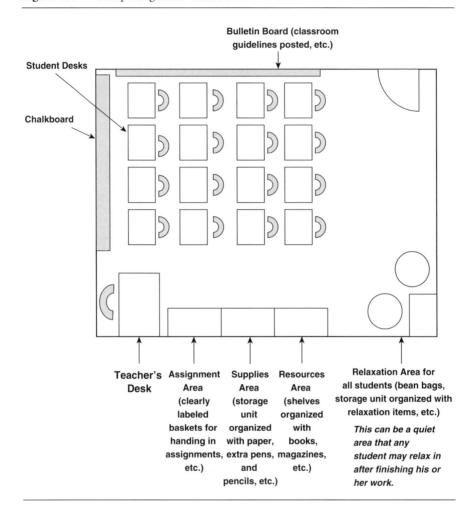

Bulletin Board (classroom guidelines posted, etc.)

Student Desks

Chalkboard

Teacher's Desk

Assignment Area (clearly labeled baskets for handing in assignments, etc.)

Supplies Area (storage unit organized with paper, extra pens, and pencils, etc.)

Resources Area (shelves organized with books, magazines, etc.)

Relaxation Area for all students (bean bags, storage unit organized with relaxation items, etc.)

This can be a quiet area that any student may relax in after finishing his or her work.

environment becomes overwhelming for him, a teacher thinks a meltdown may be on the way, or he needs a place to calm down after encountering behavioral challenges in the classroom. It is a positive place for the student, and if the student does not perceive it as such he will most likely be hesitant to use it. Home base is not a time-out, nor is it somewhere to go to escape work. The student should bring his work with him to complete while at home base.

The use of home base is an individualized process. Some students primarily use home base for coping with stress and behavioral challenges, while others use it on a regular basis to plan and review information. Time at home base can be scheduled into a student's school day and may be especially useful if scheduled following a class period or activity that proves stressful for the student with AS.

Sensory Needs

Students with AS generally have sensory needs, as discussed in the Introduction. In fact, most people, whether they have AS or not, have sensory needs. Some of us experience itchiness from the tags sewn inside clothing. Others find it difficult to concentrate when their desk is cluttered. The difference between the person without AS and the one who has AS, besides varying levels of sensitivity, is that the person without AS usually recognizes his own sensory needs and makes the necessary accommodations. For instance, he recognizes that the tags inside his shirts make his neck itch, and therefore decides to cut them out. Or she realizes that the clutter on her desk becomes too much to look at when she needs to concentrate, so she cleans her desk or moves the clutter out of view. The student with AS is often not fluent at recognizing his sensory needs in this way, much less problem-solving about ways to address them.

Once a student's sensory needs have been identified through observation, assessment, and input from the student and adults who live and work with him, they can be addressed in environments within the school. Examples of environmental modifications to a classroom based on sensory needs include the following:

- Placing materials in the classroom, such as wedge seats (wedge-shaped pieces of foam that can be placed on a student's chair), items to fidget with, and pencil grips, that allow a student to address sensory needs such as increased body awareness and additional input through touch
- Reducing the amount of visual stimuli, such as posters, in the classroom and especially in the direct line of view of a student with AS
- Arranging seating for the student with AS with her personal space preferences in mind, and arranging it to prevent the student with AS from sitting next to an area of the classroom that may easily distract her

Environmental modifications to address sensory needs do not need to be complicated or expensive. The aim is to consider the sensory needs of the student with AS and develop simple ways to address them in the various environments within the school. A little creativity goes a long way.

VISUAL SUPPORTS

Students with AS are often most successful in the classroom when they are provided with one or more types of supports. Not every student with AS will benefit from each type of support described here. Deciding which supports to provide for a student is an individualized process that should be based on information gathered from the student, members of her school team and additional service providers, and her parents, as described previously. It is also important to consider the general challenges that students with AS often have with organization, problem solving, and processing and completion time, as described in the Introduction.

Visual supports are one tool that has been shown to be effective for many individuals with autism spectrum disorders (ASD), including AS (Savner & Myles, 2000). They can benefit nonverbal and verbal individuals, as people with ASD are often visual processors. This means that information presented to them verbally is much more difficult to process than when presented visually. Even if an individual with AS has a strong ability to express himself verbally, he or she may have difficulty processing information received verbally from someone else. This becomes evident when he or she has difficulty following instructions that are presented verbally, for example. The use of visual supports to supplement or replace information that would otherwise be presented verbally can be of great assistance in such cases.

Numerous types of visual supports have been used with children with ASD, including those with AS. There are few, if any, limits to developing visual supports. The basic consideration is that a minimal amount of visual stimuli be presented.

When designing visual supports, first think about the areas in which the student would benefit from visual supports, such as understanding scheduling information, problem solving, and organization, and second determine what these supports may look like in terms of structure, age appropriateness, and so forth. The following are the main ideas to keep in mind when creating visual supports:

- Present information in a concise manner
- Include a minimal amount of visual stimuli
- Include only words OR words and pictures OR only pictures
- Make all components durable by using lamination, thick paper, etc.
- Make extra copies of all components in anticipation of lost or damaged materials
- Involve the student in making her visual supports

Schedules

Arranging scheduling information into a visual format using words and pictures serves two major purposes for the student with AS. First, it enhances students' understanding of what will occur and when, thereby accommodating their need for predictability and decreasing their anxiety about the unknown. Second, it places information that may initially have been presented verbally into a concrete visual format that strengthens students' understanding of what will occur and when. As mentioned, although many students with AS have a strong ability to express themselves verbally, they often have challenges attending to, processing, or retaining information presented to them verbally, particularly if it is not of great importance to them.

Visual schedules may be created to represent a range of information, from a student's daily schedule, to a schedule of activities that will be completed during each class period, to a schedule of the student's homework assignments for each class. The information listed in each schedule may be presented solely through words, if the student is a reader; through a combination of words and pictures; or entirely with pictures, if the student is a nonreader. Some students benefit from having a specific time frame listed on their schedules for each activity depicted, while others do better if the activities are depicted in the order in which they will occur. Again, this decision should be based on the specific student's characteristics and preferences. For example, some students with AS have challenges with rigidity and will insist on holding teachers to the specific times listed on the schedules, even if an activity accidentally runs only slightly longer or shorter than the time frame projected on the student's schedule.

Schedules should always include a disclaimer, "This schedule may change" (Moore, 2002), written so that it stands out from the other text on the schedule (e.g., in bold, in a different color, or in large letters). Students with AS often have challenges with rigidity. Changes in a schedule or routine, such as the absence of a teacher or a change from outdoor to indoor recess on the first rainy day of the fall semester, may prove quite challenging for the student with AS to cope with. This is especially true when his daily schedule tells him that he will be seeing that specific teacher that day or playing outside, not inside, at recess. It is important that the student with AS understand that changes may occur in the schedule. It is also important to notify the student of changes in the schedule as early in the day as possible, rather than leaving them as a surprise for the student to learn of as he moves from environment to environment.

How a student handles changes and the extent of flexibility he is comfortable exercising should be considered when deciding how much detail to include on any of his schedules. A sample daily schedule for Bryce, a high school freshman, has been provided in Table 2.1. He benefits from having the time for each activity listed, along with the activity name and location.

Table 2.1   Bryce's Daily Schedule

TIME	ACTIVITY	LOCATION
8:00 AM–8:10 AM	Homeroom	Room 19
8:10 AM–8:15 AM	HALL TIME	Hallway
8:15 AM–9:00 AM	Algebra	Room 25
9:00 AM–9:05 AM	HALL TIME	Hallway
9:05 AM–9:50 AM	Spanish	Room 27
9:50 AM–9:55 AM	HALL TIME	Hallway
9:55 AM–10:40 AM	Resource Room	Room 12
10:40 AM–10:45 AM	HALL TIME	Hallway
10:45 AM–11:25 AM	English	Room 31
11:25 AM–11:30 AM	HALL TIME	Hallway
11:30 AM–12:10 PM	Music	Room 10
12:10 PM–12:15 PM	HALL TIME	Hallway
12:15 PM–12:45 PM	Lunch	Cafeteria
12:45 PM–12:50 PM	HALL TIME	Hallway
12:50 PM–1:30 PM	American History	Room 6
1:30 PM–1:35 PM	HALL TIME	Hallway
1:35 PM–2:15 PM	Physical Education	Gymnasium

Lists

Lists are another valuable way to present information to students with AS. They may include information that would typically be presented only verbally, such as instructions, or not presented at all because it is assumed knowledge, such as the steps for handing in homework. Lists allow students with AS to have a concrete representation of the information to which they can refer. Lists may be written in a variety of formats, from checklists to numbered lists of the steps to take to complete a task. The following are examples of information that may be usefully presented in the form of a list:

- Teacher expectations, such as how to participate in group activities
- Routines, such as the routine for handing in homework assignments
- Steps to take to complete a task, or portion of a task, such as solving an addition problem that involves fractions with different denominators

- Reminders, such as what items a student needs to bring to play practice after school
- Choices, such as what activities a student may select from once finished with her social studies in-class assignment
- Schedule changes, such as the fact that Mr. Diaz is absent today, so a substitute teacher will be working with the students in science class, or recess will be held indoors today since it is raining too heavily to play outside
- Assignments, such as what problems the student is expected to complete that night and hand in at class tomorrow (this may also take the form of an assignment notebook)

Figure 2.4 provides examples of three types of lists: (a) steps to take to complete a task, (b) schedule changes, and (c) choices.

Figure 2.4   Types of Lists

How to Add Fractions

1. Find the least common denominator for the fractions.
2. Change all denominators to the least common denominator.
3. Multiply each numerator by the number obtained by dividing its original denominator into the least common denominator.
4. Add all numerators and write this total above the least common denominator.
5. Check my work.

Schedule Changes for Thursday, March 6

- Mr. Diaz   Mr. Diaz is not at school today. Ms. Ryan will be teaching science instead.

- Recess   It is raining, so recess will not be held outside today. It will be held inside instead.

Outside   (Inside)

Choices

After I have finished my science test during third period today, I may:

- Silently read a book of my choice at my desk until the bell rings at the end of the class period.

OR

- Go to the OT's room to relax on the swing until the bell rings at the end of the class period.

Signals and Cues

A common concern among teachers of students with AS is that these students often do not respond to teacher questions and instructions. For some students, this may be due to challenges with attention and processing of information presented verbally. Students with AS may also experience anxiety when asked a question by the teacher in front of the class and, therefore, are unresponsive or take a long time to respond to any queries in an effort to ensure that they answer correctly.

Working with the student with AS to create signals, or cues, that the teacher and student can use with each other may help the student with these challenges. For example, Laquita and Mrs. Hansen have agreed that when the class discusses the answers to assignments and Mrs. Hansen would like to call on Laquita, she will:

- Walk by Laquita's desk and tap her hand on it while saying, "Now let's talk about the answer for number three"
- Pause
- Call on Laquita to share her answer to number three from last night's homework assignment

Mrs. Hansen has not always walked up and down the aisles of her classroom while discussing assignments with her class. But she realizes the importance of preparing Laquita to share her answers with the class, so she is happy to make this small change to her typical routine. Since Mrs. Hansen walks past everyone's desk at some point and often taps her hand on a desk as she does this, it is hardly noticeable that what Mrs. Hansen seems to be doing for no specific reason actually is well-thought-out support for Laquita.

This is important to remember, as it also means that it does not automatically label Laquita to her peers as a student who needs extra help. For Laquita, the visual cue of Mrs. Hansen's hand tap prompts her to attend to what Mrs. Hansen is about to say. Mrs. Hansen's concise verbal cue, "Now let's talk about the answer for number three," is addressed to the entire class, but Laquita knows that is her cue to look at her assignment for her answer to this question. Mrs. Hansen's pause gives Laquita the time to process what Mrs. Hansen has just said and to locate her answer to the question. She is then ready to share it with the class when Mrs. Hansen subsequently calls on her. Laquita has successfully attended to an instruction and answered a question, without any feelings of anxiety or embarrassment on her part.

Maps

Maps provide students with a visual representation of their environment that can help them remember where places and people are. Maps can also be labeled to help students remember when they will visit places or people on a map. Again, this provides structure and helps students orient to their surroundings. A sample map of a student's school hallways appears in Figure 2.5.

Figure 2.5   Sample School Map

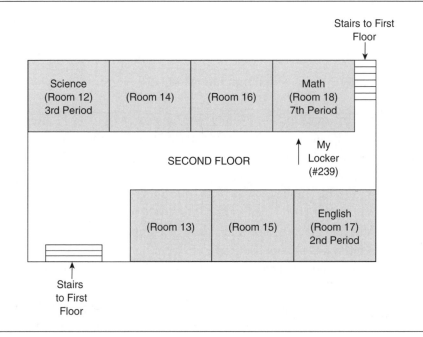

ORGANIZATIONAL STRATEGIES

While all students can benefit from learning to use organizational strategies, for students with AS it is essential for their school team to help them develop these strategies, given the challenges these students often experience with organization. Organization is generally considered in two broad categories: organization of time and organization of space (Morgenstern & Morgenstern-Colón, 2002). For students, their time at school mainly consists of the daily schedule and the schedule within each class period. Their space, in turn, largely consists of their desk, locker, and backpack.

Three-Phrase Process

Organization of a student's time and space can be broken down into three phases for each organizational task: (a) analyze, (b) strategize, and (c) attack space (Morgenstern & Morgenstern-Colón, 2002). In the first phase, students answer four questions that help them in *analyzing* the organizational task.

1. What is and is not working in their current method of organization in this area?

2. What are the seven (to pinpoint a reasonable, but not excessive amount) most important items in the area they will be organizing?

3. What is the benefit, or payoff, of organizing the area?

4. What is the problem(s) that has caused disorganization in this area?

All of these questions are important for any student to answer who wants to organize an area of his time or space. However, question 3 is of particular interest for the student with AS who may not understand why organization of his time and space is important, as to him it is not a priority. Further, due to his challenges, he does not understand why organization would be important to anyone else, like his teacher or peers. But his teacher, who is the recipient of the student's crumpled papers, or the locker mate who often has papers fluttering out onto her from the student's disorganized locker, definitely feels organization skills should be his priority. In addressing question 3 then, it is important to find a way to make organization meaningful to the student with AS. This may be accomplished through means such as the use of Power Cards (discussed in Chapter 5) with a role model who shares his tips for organization with the student with AS.

The second phase of organization is to *strategize*. This involves keeping in mind a visual representation of the well-organized classroom and the principles it encompasses. Based on these concepts, the student can develop her own visual map of what the time or space she will be organizing will look like when she is finished. The student should also consider how much time it will take her to complete the organizational task, being careful not to under- or overestimate the amount of time required to complete a task. A misestimate of time can lead to frustration. Reasonable estimates for some school-related organization tasks include:

- School Papers: 2–3 hours
- Backpack: 1/2–1 hour
- Locker: 1/2–1 hour
- Schedule: 1–2 hours (Morgenstern & Morgenstern-Colón, 2002)

The third step to the organization process is to *attack*. Organizational tools, supplies, and strategies are used to help the student organize his time and space. The four components of attacking the organization of time can be remembered through the acronym WADE:

- **W**rite down information about tasks that have to be completed in a medium such as a planner.
- **A**dd the amount of time that it will take to complete the tasks. Break large tasks down into a series of smaller ones.
- **D**ecide when to complete each task, with an emphasis on prioritizing tasks so that the most important ones are completed first.
- **E**xecute a plan for completing each task, avoiding the pitfalls of procrastination and perfectionism.

The five components of attacking organization of space can be remembered through the acronym SPACE:

- **S**ort items, grouping similar ones together.
- **P**urge any items that are not needed, are duplicates, and so on.
- **A**ssign a place to store each item that will be kept.
- **C**ontainerize, using a variety of storage materials such as file cabinets, bins, and baskets to store items, keeping them well organized and making cleanup an easier task.
- **E**qualize, gaining new items and removing old ones as one's interests, goals, and needs change over time. (Morgenstern & Morgenstern-Colón, 2002).

Figure 2.6 provides an example of how one student with AS, Maya, worked with her teacher to use the three-phase process to organize her desk.

Figure 2.6   Maya's Three-Step Organizational Strategy

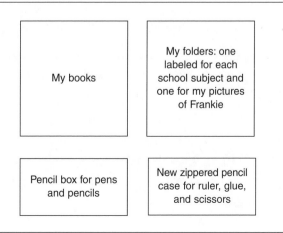

Three-Step Organizational Strategy

Analyze

1. What is and is not working in your current method of organization in this area?

   Is Working:
   - have a pencil box in my desk for storing small items such as pens, pencils, and scissors
   - have folders in my desk where I can keep all of the papers for my school subjects

   Is Not Working:
   - have pens and pencils scattered throughout my desk, not just in my pencil box
   - my papers are usually stuffed into one or two out of the seven folders that I have or they are loose in my desk
   - do not have anywhere to keep things like my ruler, glue, and pictures of Frankie Muniz

2. What are the seven (to pinpoint a reasonable, but not excessive amount) most important items in the area you will be organizing?
   a. Books
   b. Papers
   c. Pens and pencils
   d. Scissors
   e. Ruler
   f. Glue
   g. Personal items such as pictures of Frankie

3. What is the benefit, or payoff, of organizing the area?

   I will be able to find items when I need to hand them in, refer to them, or use them in any other way just like Frankie Muniz does when he is tutored on the *Malcolm in the Middle* set.

4. What is the problem(s) that has caused disorganization in this area?

   I am not very good at deciding how to organize my things and sticking with any ideas I put into place.

Strategize

Time Estimate: I think this will take me about 2 1/2 hours to organize. I need to sort through all of my papers and pictures and put them into the right folder. This might take a while.

Attack

- **S**ort items, grouping similar ones together.

    I stayed after school one day and took the contents of my desk to the back of the classroom where we have a big open floor space. I sat on the floor and organized my papers and pictures by placing them into each of the folders I now had labeled for them. I then placed my pens and pencils into my pencil box and my ruler, glue, and scissors into my zippered pencil case.

- **P**urge any items that are not needed, are duplicates, and so on.

    It turns out that I had more than one copy of many of my school papers. This is probably because I usually couldn't find the papers I needed so my teacher would give me another copy. When I organized everything I threw out all of the extra copies.

- **A**ssign a place to store each item that will be kept.

    I already did this when I drew my picture of what the inside of my desk could look like. My teacher helped me think about how we could design this—I would have had a hard time doing this by myself.

- **C**ontainerize, using a variety of storage materials such as file cabinets, bins, and baskets to store items, keeping them well organized and making cleanup an easier task.

    I used folders, my pencil box, and a zippered pencil case to help organize the items I have.

- **E**qualize, gaining new items and removing old ones as one's interests, goals, and needs change over time.

    I'll be doing this in the future—for now, I am all set! My teacher and I have agreed to meet to review how I am doing with the organization of my desk at least one time per quarter.

SUMMARY

Students with AS demonstrate a number of unique characteristics and challenges that can be accommodated through various environmental modifications and supports. All modifications and supports should be individualized to meet a specific student's strengths, challenges, interests, goals, and learning style, rather than only taking into account the general characteristics and needs of students with AS. Further, an emphasis should be placed on the student's strengths, rather than his challenges, and these strengths should be built upon when possible. Structure, predictability, consistency, and flexibility should also be prime considerations in developing modifications and supports. While the student with AS may initially be supported in this process, the team's long-term goal should be to help him gain independence in recognizing the areas in which he needs supports and modifications and learning to ask for these to be implemented. This is also true of academic supports and modifications, as will be discussed in the next chapter.

Academic Modifications

3

with Anastasia Hubbard

CASE STUDY: KHALID

Khalid is in several inclusive classes. He has a special interest in tornadoes and enjoys talking about how they form, where they most often occur in the United States, and what kind of damage they may cause. Khalid was experiencing challenges at school in a number of academic areas and skills, so his teachers decided to try incorporating his interest in tornadoes into some of his academic activities. They aimed to integrate Khalid's interest into all stages of the learning process, including being presented with information, organizing and learning information, and demonstrating knowledge of information.

Developed by: Jeanne Holverstott

Students with AS usually have average to above-average intelligence quotients (IQs), with some students having IQs in the superior or very superior range (Barnhill, Hagiwara, Myles, & Simpson, 2000). As pointed out earlier, while these students are intelligent, they face unique challenges that often require academic modifications to enable them to reach their full potential in the school environment. Academic modifications refer to alterations made to academic activities to address the strengths, challenges, interests, goals, and learning styles of the student with AS. In other words, they are based on information gathered through observations, interviews, and assessments, as described in Chapter 2, and summarized in a student's Snapshot of Learner Characteristics.

This chapter describes specific academic modifications that may be beneficial for the student with AS. Figure 3.1 is a visual representation of the way in which these modifications have been organized in this chapter. First, two key areas of challenge will be identified—reliance on predictability

Figure 3.1   Visual Representation of This Chapter's Organization of Academic Modifications

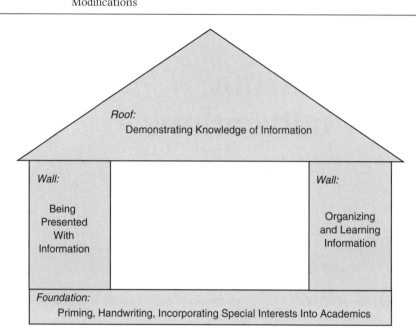

and handwriting skills—followed by a discussion of the benefits of incorporating a student's special interest into his academics. These areas often provide the foundation for the student's academics and for the next area that will be covered, stages of the learning process. The first two stages of the learning process are (a) being presented with information and (b) organizing and learning information. These stages are like walls that are supported by the foundation of predictability, handwriting, and special interests and that provide additional support for the roof, demonstrating knowledge of information. This roof overarches the learning process, as this is the stage where it becomes evident what level of proficiency the student has developed in an academic area. This level of proficiency also provides feedback as to whether or not the strategies put into place (the foundation and walls) have helped the student to develop his skills in this area.

PREDICTABILITY AND HANDWRITING

Priming

Priming a student means preparing her for an activity that she will be expected to complete (Myles & Adreon, 2001). Priming allows the student to preview information or activities that she will be presented with in the near future in an effort to (a) accommodate her preference for predictability and (b) promote her success with these activities. With the emphasis placed on previewing activities before they will occur, the student is often less likely to experience anxiety and stress about what lies ahead. With anxiety and stress at a minimum, the student can focus her efforts on successfully completing activities.

Priming is not a time for teaching the academic content of activities or making sure the student has learned it. The actual materials that will be used in an activity, such as a worksheet or outline for a group project, may be shown to the student during priming so she knows what she will be working on in an upcoming class. However, the student is not asked to complete the worksheet at this time. It is strictly a preview. Schedules of events or lists may also be used during priming. They may depict a series of events that will occur or information that will be covered during an upcoming activity.

Priming should occur close to when the target activity will occur. For example, priming may take place the day before an activity, the morning of it, the class period before, or even at the beginning of the class period during which the activity will be completed. Anyone can help the student with priming, from a teacher to a parent to a peer. Priming should occur in short, concise time periods in an environment that is relaxing for the student with AS, and with a person who is patient and supportive (Myles & Adreon, 2001).

Handwriting and the Student With AS

The majority of students with AS have challenges with fine-motor skills, including handwriting (Myles, Huggins, Rome-Lake, Hagiwara, Barnhill, & Griswold, 2003). Teachers of students with AS often describe concerns with these students' handwriting itself as well as the students' feelings towards handwriting, such as:

- Using large-size characters, particularly for older students
- Exhibiting sloppiness and illegibility of handwriting, in general
- Using extensive time to complete tasks requiring handwriting
- Dislike of, or even refusal to complete, tasks that require handwriting

For anyone unfamiliar with the characteristics of AS, or anyone unaware that a student has AS, the latter two characteristics may be perceived as inappropriate, noncompliant behavior. However, this is rarely the case for the student with AS. Handwriting may, in fact, be an uncomfortable (even painful) and emotionally and physically draining process for the student with AS due to fine-motor challenges, similar to completing a two-mile hike when suffering from arthritis in the knees.

The school team working with a student with AS must ensure that they consider any challenges the student may experience with handwriting and make appropriate modifications. Sample accommodations include, but are not limited to

- Asking a student to only write key words in response to a question, rather than writing complete sentences
- Modifying assignments and tests to incorporate multiple-choice, fill-in-the-blank, matching, and/or short-answer questions, rather than essay questions
- Letting the student underline or highlight answers to questions in a reading passage, rather than having to write out the answers
- Allowing the student to use a computer or personal digital assistant (PDA) to type information, rather than write it by hand
- Permitting the student to verbally express information and tape record it, rather than write it by hand
- Allowing the student to verbally express information to a person, who will serve as a scribe, writing down all of the information the student with AS says
- Asking the student with AS to first generate a handwritten or typed list of key points which he will then formulate into his verbal answers, perhaps using one of the graphic organizers discussed in this chapter

Keyboarding should be taught from an early age to students with AS, so that they have the opportunity to become proficient in typing. While handwriting is emphasized throughout the school years, as the student becomes older and enters high school, college, and the working world, he most likely will not be required to use handwriting, other than to provide a legal signature. If he is a proficient typist, he should have no difficulty recording information in a written (typewritten) format.

In summary, it is imperative to remember that using informal or formal assessments involving handwriting is not an appropriate way to find out what a student with AS knows. Modifications such as those previously described should be used instead to truly tap into the student's knowledge and abilities.

INCORPORATING THE STUDENT'S
INTERESTS INTO THE CURRICULUM

As mentioned earlier, intense—sometimes all-consuming—attention to specific areas of interest is a major characteristic of students with AS.

Students with AS tend to enjoy learning more about their special interests and are motivated by them. Incorporating them into the curriculum is one way to make interesting a task that may initially seem overwhelming or lacking in meaning to a student with AS.

This proved true for Khalid, whose interest in tornadoes was previously described. For example, Khalid's math teacher, Mrs. Chen, developed activities that required Khalid to calculate items such as a tornado's speed, and based on that, the number of miles it traveled between its touchdown and retreat. His science teacher, Ms. Slowinski, created activities that enabled Khalid to further study the weather conditions necessary for a tornado to form. Based on this, and additional information collected, Khalid completed a project describing why tornadoes occur more frequently in some areas of the United States than others. Further, Mr. Carey, Khalid's social studies teacher, provided Khalid with readings on significant tornado events in history. This gave Khalid opportunities to practice a number of skills, including: (a) completing the readings, (b) identifying and taking notes on each section's main idea and key points, and (c) creating visual representations of information learned to demonstrate his knowledge of the material. One means of assessment for this unit of study was the creation of a timeline of significant tornado events in history, which enabled Khalid to practice his sequencing skills. A second means of assessment for this unit of study involved making a map of the United States on the computer, including color-coding states based on the frequency of tornadoes and identifying and labeling locations of the significant tornado events Khalid read about. This allowed Khalid to practice his geography skills.

In general, Khalid displayed enthusiasm for completing these academic assignments that incorporated his interest in tornadoes. For example, when he encountered the demand for skills that tend to prove difficult for him, such as identifying a reading's main ideas and key points, Khalid did not immediately withdraw and refuse to complete the assignment, as often occurred with material that was of little interest to him. Instead, he wanted to learn what the reading described about tornadoes. He knew, though, that in order to continue to read and learn more about tornadoes, he first had to stop after each paragraph and identify its main idea and key point. Mr. Carey had clearly described this to him through the use of a learning contract when priming Khalid for this assignment.

Khalid did not necessarily breeze through these social studies reading assignments. However, because the content—tornadoes—was an interest of his and proved motivating and reinforcing, he progressed with greater enthusiasm, compliance, and desire to ask for help when needed. He also experienced less anxiety than usual. This may be because, due to his interest in the material, he was able to focus on the difficult parts of the task, rather than also having to focus on making it through a reading he found uninteresting.

Most people are, at least occasionally, asked or required to complete tasks that do not incorporate their interests. Most juniors or seniors in high school, for example, have to prepare to take the SATs or ACTs, something few of them would describe as interesting and enjoyable. These students can progress through the necessary phases of studying because they have some knowledge base for planning and organizing their study time and materials, as well as breaking them down into manageable components. Even though some material covered by the SATs and ACTs is more difficult than others for a student with AS she can create a plan for approaching and learning the more difficult material. If she becomes frustrated or anxious as she progresses with her studying, most likely she will have the skills to problem solve, perhaps deciding to either ask someone for help or to take a break for a day and enjoy a leisure activity instead.

These steps of planning, organizing, and problem solving are areas that are of minimal difficulty for most people, but for individuals with AS they can be extremely challenging, as described throughout this book. When faced not only with material that does not interest him, but also the steps of organizing, planning, problem solving, and perhaps even specific academic skills that are difficult for him, a student with AS may become bogged down in the details and, as a result, become worried and anxious. This makes it even more challenging for him to complete the related project.

As a result, one must first focus on helping the student with AS enhance the skills that are necessary to complete his academic work, such as planning, organizing, and problem solving. Incorporating his special interest into this enables him to focus solely on those skills, which most likely will reduce his worry and anxiety, while also building an interest and positive reinforcement for him. As the student becomes stronger at these skills, the special interest can gradually be faded from use, and other topics added in its place. The student will now be able to focus more energy on approaching new content because he is more comfortable and has to devote less energy to skills such as planning, organizing, and problem solving.

STAGES OF THE LEARNING PROCESS

Being Presented With Information

As described previously, students with AS often have difficulty attending to information presented verbally and then processing it. For any student with these difficulties, modifications should be made to enable the student to be successful at following instructions. Instinct often prompts someone to say the student's name before giving an instruction and to speak a little louder as well. While this may work for students who do not have AS, it most likely will not prove effective for students with AS. For these students, modifications for gaining student attention and presenting instructions include:

- Establishing the student's attention through a visual cue (tap on her desk, place a picture prompt in front of her, etc.)
- Presenting the instruction in a concise verbal statement (for instance, "Please stand up now.")
- Considering following the presentation of a verbal instruction with a visual prompt (for instance, a picture symbol for "stand up")

Instructions may also be presented largely through visual means. Depending on the student, this may occur through the use of written words, a combination of picture symbols and words, or solely picture symbols, as mentioned in the visual supports section of Chapter 2. Even when presented visually, instructions should be presented concisely, explicitly, and in a step-by-step format because the student with AS usually has difficulty problem solving and may not naturally consider a component of an instruction that students without AS would usually infer.

Consider the wording of instructions as well, taking into account that a student with AS may interpret the instructions quite literally. Aim to avoid any wording that may confuse the student. Table 3.1 depicts examples of instructions that are worded well for a student with AS, compared to versions of the same instructions that are worded poorly for this student.

Organizing and Learning Information

Graphic Organizers

Since students with AS may have difficulty processing information and problem solving, it can be challenging for them to take in information presented through class activities and assignments and put it into a meaningful context. This becomes evident when a student has read a chapter on southwestern United States, for instance, but does not know where to begin when completing his assignment, which involves writing a summary of the key points of the chapter. Graphic organizers are valuable tools for helping students with AS organize important information about a topic in a manner that suits their tendency to be visual learners.

Graphic organizers are available through a number of means, including paper templates, downloads from Web sites, and as components of computer programs. They can also be generated by hand. Graphic

Table 3.1   Presenting Instructions to the Student With AS

Educator's Instruction	Student's Possible Interpretation(s)	Suggestion for Rewording (consider presenting these with a visual format)
"Do this worksheet."	What do I "do" with it? When do I "do" it? Do I have to get it all done during this class period? I don't have enough time to do all of this.	"Here are 5 addition problems. You can work on them in any order you want. If we don't finish them all today, that's okay."
After encountering a challenging math problem, educator says, "Put your thinking cap on."	I don't have a thinking hat. I don't even wear hats. And besides, you can't wear hats in school anyway. That's the rule.	"Let's think about how to solve this problem. What should we do first?" (Continue step-by-step through the process of solving the math problem with the student.)
"Finish your spelling list and turn it in."	What do you mean by "finish it"? What do you want me to do? Where do I turn it in when I am done?	"You have 10 spelling words this week. Type one sentence for each word. Use the spelling word in the sentence. Then put your spelling papers in the red spelling basket on our assignments table."

organizers may take a variety of formats, but can generally be classified into four types: (a) sequential, (b) cyclical, (c) conceptual, and (d) hierarchical (Bromley, Irwin-DeVitis, & Modio, 1995).

Sequential graphic organizers provide a visual representation of a series of events such as a timeline (see Figure 3.2) or cause and effect (see Figure 3.3). Cyclical graphic organizers describe events with no beginning, middle, or end, such as the life cycle of an organism (see Figure 3.4). Conceptual graphic organizers begin with one key concept, as described by one word or phrase, and enable supporting ideas to be depicted as branches off the key concept (see Figure 3.5). They are grouped by idea, but are not necessarily listed in a specific order, serving as more of a brainstorm related to a topic. Hierarchical graphic organizers can also provide a concise visual representation of key concepts and their supporting concepts and ideas, but enable this information to be described in a linear manner (see Figure 3.6). Another graphic organizer, The Unit Organizer (Lenz, Bulgren, Schumaker, Deshler, & Boudah, 1994), can be used to tie information from a unit of study together into one document. A template has been provided for The Unit Organizer (see Figure 3.7) as well as a sample Unit Organizer (Figure 3.8).

Figure 3.2 Lewis and Clark Expedition Timeline

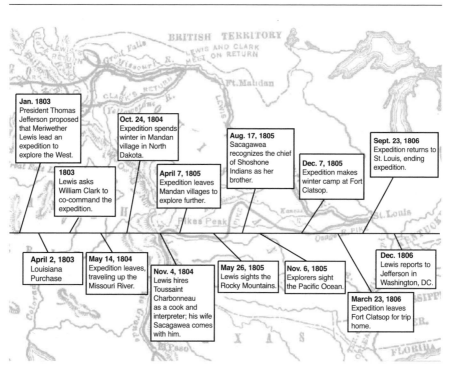

Developed by: Spencer Nolan. Reprinted by permission.

Figure 3.3 Cause and Effect

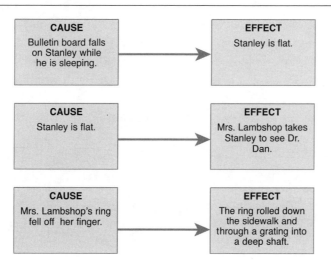

Developed by: Spencer Nolan. Reprinted by permission.

Figure 3.4   Cyclical Graphic Organizer

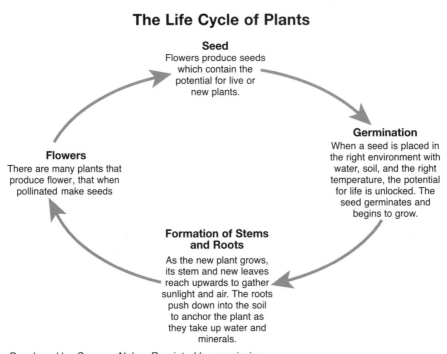

Developed by: Spencer Nolan. Reprinted by permission.

Figure 3.5   Conceptual Graphic Organizer

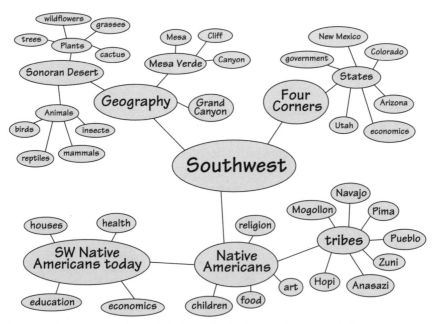

Developed by: Spencer Nolan and Heather Tillinghast. Reprinted by permission.

Figure 3.6   Hierarchical Graphic Organizer

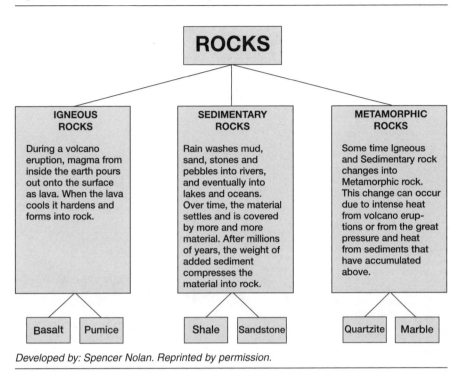

Developed by: Spencer Nolan. Reprinted by permission.

Figure 3.7   Unit Organizer

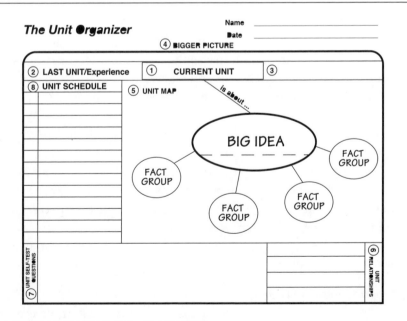

Lenz (1994). Used and adapted with permission.

Figure 3.8   Sample Unit Organizer

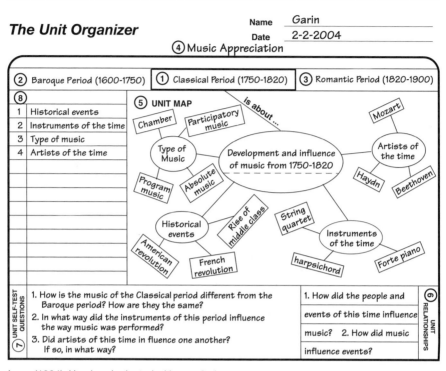

Lenz (1994). Used and adapted with permission.

Note-Taking Strategies

Students receive information on new academic material from two main sources—readings and presentations (i.e., lectures, videos). Students with AS may benefit from modifications that help them process this information, synthesize it, and record aspects that are most important to remember.

Most students use note taking to help process, synthesize, and record information shared in readings and presentations. However, note taking in itself is a complex task. It requires students to attend to the written or verbal information before them, consider its message, decide what information is most important to remember, and determine how to record this information for future reference. Students with AS may have difficulty with note taking not only because of the skill demands, but also because of the following challenges typically experienced by individuals with AS:

- Fine-motor skills, such as writing
- Visual motor skills, such as being able to easily alternate eye gaze back and forth between a textbook or the blackboard and a sheet of paper for writing notes on

- Slow processing time for considering and recording information presented verbally
- Inability to determine the main ideas and key points of information being presented
- Difficulty selecting a way to record information in a clear, concise manner that will be meaningful to refer to in the future when studying for tests

As a result, note-taking modifications are necessary and may include the following:

- Supplying the student with a teacher-made outline of main ideas and key points from readings and presentations
- Giving the student a teacher-made outline of main ideas, each of which is followed by clearly labeled areas for the student to contribute key points
- Providing the student with visual learning software to use or handouts with blank graphic organizers to help record and organize information
- Having someone else (for instance, a peer or paraprofessional) record information for the student. A peer's notes can be photocopied and shared with the student with AS, or carbon paper may be used to make a duplicate copy as the peer creates the notes
- Tape recording information presented verbally to enable the student to take notes at his own pace and refer back to the tape recording as needed

In preparation for note taking, it may be necessary to teach a student with AS how to identify main ideas and key points of information. This is important because some students with AS may become too focused on the details of the information being presented, sometimes to the exclusion of the main concepts. It may be most beneficial to initially teach this skill based on visually presented information, such as readings, not only because students with AS tend to be visual processors as previously discussed, but also because it allows them to refer back to the information being presented. Through means such as direct instruction, students can be asked to read a paragraph and then identify its main idea, followed by additional key points. Assistance can be provided as necessary to aid the student in understanding how to select main ideas and key points, with the goal that the student becomes increasingly independent at accomplishing this task.

Specific note-taking strategies, called Coffee Breaks, have been used with students with AS (Moore, 2002). Four strategies are described—Half

Figure 3.9   Half and Half Note-Taking Method on American Symbols

Book Notes	Class Notes
Symbol • Something that stands for something else • America has three symbols for freedom	**Symbol**
Liberty Bell • In Philadelphia • Rung when Declaration of Independence was read in 1776 • Cracked two times, not repaired • Reminds Americans of freedom from England	**Liberty Bell**
American Flag • 1st flag had 13 stars and 13 stripes • Now flag has 13 stripes and 50 stars • Reminds people of freedom in America	**American Flag**
Statue of Liberty • Given to America in 1886 (gift from France) • In New York Harbor • Symbol of freedom to people who come to America	**Statue of Liberty**

Developed by: Susan Thompson Moore

and Half, Cream and Sugar, Decaf, and Instant. When using Half and Half, students first divide their paper into two sections by folding the paper in half vertically. On one half of the paper notes can be recorded from readings, while on the other half notes can be recorded from in-class presentations. Colored pencils may be used to write headings such as main ideas or key words on each half of the paper, with key points listed below headings in point form. This is a concise, clearly organized method to record and compare information obtained from two different sources. Using the Cream and Sugar method of note taking, students are assisted by another person, such as their teacher or paraprofessional, to identify and record main ideas and key points. The Decaf method incorporates less writing on a student's part by requiring that he complete an entire reading but only take notes on a portion of it. The remainder of the reading's notes are supplied to the student. Finally, the Instant method requires even less writing as notes are provided for the student in their entirety. Figure 3.9 is a sample of the Half and Half method that Jin's teacher helped her develop during a social studies unit on American symbols.

Deciding which note-taking modifications and strategies to use is an individualized process based on the specific student's strengths and challenges. It may also require some trial and error. A student and her teacher should try different modifications and strategies until finding the one(s) that provides the student with an adequate level of support.

Demonstrating Knowledge of Material

All students should be given the flexibility to demonstrate their knowledge in a variety of ways. Some students are strong test takers, while others perform best when asked to write a paper. Some students enjoy using their creativity to express their knowledge, preferring to make a video, write a story, or make a poster to express what they know. Students with AS are no different, but they also have challenges with fine-motor skills (especially handwriting), anxiety, and stress that should be considered when making assignments.

Assignments, Projects, and Tests

When considering methods of determining student competence, such as assignments, projects, and tests, the following aspects are usually taken into consideration for students with AS: (a) individualization, (b) format, (c) completion, and (d) follow-up.

Individualization. Individualization involves allowing students to demonstrate their knowledge of material using means that are best suited to their strengths, challenges, interests, goals, and learning styles. As previously described, one student may need to have her knowledge of a topic assessed through written papers, while another may perform best on tests, and yet another may best show her skills giving a presentation. While all students benefit from these types of opportunities for individualization, it is especially important for students with AS. Thus, the challenges they face in areas such as fine-motor skills, planning, organizing, literal thinking, and problem solving merit alternative means of assessment that will allow them to accurately demonstrate their knowledge and to do so with minimal anxiety. The following is a list of ideas for ways students can demonstrate their knowledge on a topic:

- Papers
- Tests
- Oral presentation
- Video presentation
- Bulletin board display
- Creating a short book
- Helping another student learn about the topic
- Writing a story or poem
- Drawing or painting a picture
- Tape recording a mock radio broadcast
- Writing a song

- Acting out information
- Creating puzzles (e.g., making a word search or crossword puzzle)
- Designing and making posters
- Making a board game
- Making a collage
- Creating a newsletter
- Writing a letter
- Making a Web page

Format. Format involves all aspects of an assignment, project, or test, including length, layout, types of questions, and how important information, such as instructions, will be shared with students. For students with AS, the following is important to consider in relation to each of these aspects:

- *Length.* Methods of assessment should be concise and correlate with the student's abilities (i.e., avoid creating a method of assessment that will be too long, and therefore potentially overwhelming for the student with AS to complete). In particular, a student's handwriting abilities and typical amount of processing time needed to complete an activity should be considered.

- *Layout.* Aim to present methods of assessment in a clear, concise visual format. The amount of information and number of assessment items included on a page should be kept to a minimum. Providing a student with too much information at once may distract her visually and prevent her from being able to focus on the most important information on each page. For some students, it may also be beneficial to use pictures to accompany words in an effort to make the information more concrete. Consider using a larger font size.

- *Types of questions.* Two aspects of designing assessment questions should be considered. First, the amount of handwriting required to answer a question needs to be reviewed. Students with AS who experience fine-motor challenges that make handwriting difficult may benefit from the use of oral assessments; written questions presented in multiple-choice, fill-in-the-blank, matching, or short-answer format; and/or the option of using a computer or scribe to answer questions that require long answers. Second, the clarity of questions must be considered. Questions should be concise and be evaluated for explicitness, taking into account that students with AS often have challenges with pinpointing the most important information in a reading selection, and being flexible in their thinking, besides having a tendency to interpret information literally. For instance, true/false questions can be extremely challenging for a student with AS as they require the student to select the most important words in a sentence to determine its validity. A student with AS may spend too much time trying to interpret the statements and may have difficulty determining which information in the sentence is the most important to focus on when deciding if the statement is true or false (Moore, 2002).

- *How important information will be shared.* Students with AS may benefit from having important information, such as the written instructions for an assignment, project, or test, explicitly conveyed to them. Highlighting the relevant text can be effective.

Completion. Completion involves all of the steps a student, teacher, or paraprofessional takes once a method of assessment is created. For most students, this involves the teacher providing them with the relevant material, reviewing instructions, clarifying questions, and then having students complete and return the assignment, project, or test. For students with AS, additional steps may be required:

- *Preparation.* The student should be briefed on and prepared for the upcoming method of assessment through priming (discussed earlier in this chapter). Priming may also include providing the student with a contract or a model for the assignment, project, or test.

- *Contracts* enable a teacher and student to work together to agree upon and clearly outline the expectations, options, and outcomes for a student when completing an academic task. Most students with AS benefit from the use of contracts because they provide them with structure, predictability, and a visual representation of the task at hand. Contracts incorporate another visual support discussed in this chapter—lists—as they may include lists of (a) components of a task that can be checked off as the student completes each one, (b) choices for activities to complete as components of the academic task, and (c) guidelines about expectations for the task or the student's environment while completing it. Figure 3.10 is a sample contract.

- Providing students with AS with a *model* of an assignment or project helps them understand what is expected of them. By giving them structure and predictability for the task at hand, the use of models often reduces anxiety for the student. A model is a completed version of the assignment or project, often illustrating the standards for gaining a letter grade of "A." Given to the student with AS prior to beginning an assignment or project,

Figure 3.10   Sample Contract

Contract

Student Name: _____ Nihar _____ **Date:** _____ 1/22/04 _____

Subject: _____ Social Studies _____ **Assignment:** _____ World Map Project _____

Tasks:

Please write a check mark in each box as you complete the task written next to it. You may complete these tasks in any order.

❑ Label all continents on the world map that you have been given.

❑ Label all oceans on the world map that you have been given.

❑ On your world map, place an asterisk on, and label the location of, each of the geographic features listed on the attached list. (This list is labeled "World Map Project – Geographic Features.")

❑ On your world map, place an asterisk on, and label the location of, each of the cities listed on the attached list. (This list is labeled "World Map Project – Cities.")

❑ On your world map, find the location of each of the person-made features that are listed on the attached list. (This list is labeled "World Map Project – Person-Made Features.) Next to each location's name, write the name of the person-made feature that is located there.

When you have **finished** these steps, choose which one (1) of the following three (3) additional activities you will also complete for this project. Please draw a circle around the choice number that you select.

Choice #1: Choose one of the cities that you labeled on your world map. Write a paragraph about what types of things you might see if you lived there.

Choice #2: Choose one of the cities that you labeled on your world map. Make a video about what types of things you might see if you lived there.

Choice #3: Choose one of the cities that you labeled on your world map. Tape record a pretend radio broadcast discussing what types of things you might see if you lived there.

Guidelines:

- Project Due Date: February 16, 2004
- If you do not understand a part of, or an entire, instruction written above, ask your teacher to help explain it to you.
- You have been given a model of what this assignment should look like when you are finished with it. This is an example that will give you an idea of what a project that would receive a letter grade of "A" may look like.

_____   _____
         Teacher's Signature   Student's Signature

---

it offers her a visual representation that concretely demonstrates how to complete the task and what a finished product may look like. She can then concentrate on the content of the assignment or project, rather than also having to be concerned about how to format it.

- *Teach the format.* Teaching the student how to complete the assignment, project, or test before asking him to complete it himself is essential. This includes teaching the student how to answer multiple-choice questions or how to write a book report.

- *Assess task-related sensory needs.* Take into account a student's sensory needs before he begins an in-class assignment, project, or test. For example, one student may work best when allowed to complete a test in a quiet room by himself because he is sensitive to sounds in his environment. Another student may be able to complete an assignment in her classroom, but she may have difficulty writing unless a slant board (a wedge-shaped block of wood, similar in shape to the top of a podium) is placed on her desk for support when writing.

- *Reinforce progress throughout.* The student should receive reinforcement throughout the completion of tests, projects, or assignments through social praise and tangible reinforcers such as stickers. Some students may benefit from having a teacher or paraprofessional simply check off each component of the assignment, project, or test on its associated document, as the student completes it (Moore, 2002; Myles & Adreon, 2001).

- *Check in with the student.* The teacher should be in constant contact with the student as she completes the assignment, project, or test to ensure that she is making adequate progress and, if she is not, take time to clarify any aspects of the assessment as needed.

- *Monitor student understanding.* The student should be asked to explain or paraphrase to the teacher or paraprofessional what he is expected to do. If the student does not demonstrate a clear comprehension of the assignment, project, or test, the relevant adult can help him strengthen that understanding.

- *Allow breaks.* The student should be encouraged to take a break when needed when taking a test or even when sitting at his desk for a lengthy period of time to complete a worksheet.

- *Complete on-the-spot adjustments.* Teachers and paraprofessionals who work with students with AS should aim to consistently be aware of whether such aspects as the rate of presentation of material, length of assessment, and location of assessment are working well for the student.

If one or more of these aspects is not working well, the teacher or para-professional should be flexible enough to implement a modification or support to aid the student at that particular time. For example, if a student is having difficulty comprehending the instructions for an assignment, his paraprofessional might write a numbered list that concisely lists each step the student has to take to complete the assignment and that includes a hand-drawn picture to help the student visualize each step.

- *Follow-up.* Follow-up includes all of the steps taken once a student has completed an assignment, a project, or test and primarily includes providing reinforcement, creating opportunities for repetition, and checking for generalization and maintenance of skills.

- *Provide positive reinforcement.* All students should receive positive reinforcement for effort and achievement on assessments. Some students with AS may need more frequent reinforcement, as well as more tangible, or even interest-specific, reinforcement.

- *Enable opportunities for repetition.* Students with AS may learn some information particularly quickly, such as rote facts, especially if they pertain to their special interest. But in general, students with ASD, including AS, benefit from being provided with opportunities for repetition when learning material.

- *Check for generalization and maintenance of skills.* Generalization refers to the ability to learn information in one environment and with one person or a group of people, and then be able to apply the same information to a different environment or person(s). Since individuals with AS often have difficulty in this area, it is important to check for generalization. Maintenance involves using a skill over time and keeping it in one's repertoire. Students may be taught some information that they are not expected to remember in detail forever, such as the list of all of the presidents of the United States. However, they will also be taught information that they will be expected to remember forever, such as how to solve addition, subtraction, multiplication, and division problems. All students benefit from maintenance checks to determine that they are still able to complete designated tasks.

The most important factor to keep in mind when creating and implementing methods of assessment can most simply be called "the big picture." Consider what the long-term goals are for the student and create assignments, projects, or tests that will best help her reach them. For example, if a student has difficulty with handwriting and identifying main ideas and she is preparing for an English test on *The Great Gatsby*, it should be considered whether the goal is for the student to develop greater proficiency in handwriting or in identifying main ideas. For this assignment, the big picture involves whether or not the student can identify main ideas after completing a reading assignment. Ensuring that the student supplies these main ideas through handwriting like the other students in her class is not a part of the big picture. She can demonstrate her knowledge of main ideas equally well through typewritten or verbal means and should be allowed to do so given her challenges with handwriting.

Table 3.2 is a checklist of modifications to be considered when making academic modifications for students with AS, largely summarizing the modifications discussed in this chapter. It is crucial to note that these modifications should also be considered and applied when preparing for and actually taking national, state, or local proficiency exams. These modifications can be built upon and tweaked as needed in order to fit exam guidelines.

Table 3.2   Sample Modifications to Consider

Key Information to Consider: What is the "big picture"? In other words, what is the goal for a specific student for a specific task or topic?

Building the Foundation for Learning

❑ Complete priming with student

❑ Design assignments, projects, and tests that only include as much handwriting as is appropriate to student's abilities

❑ Incorporate student's interests into academic activities

Presenting, Organizing, and Learning Information

❑ Provide instructions that are concise, explicit, and step by step

- May include verbal instructions
- Consider following up/supplementing any verbal instructions with visual supports (e.g., a list of the steps the student should complete in order to finish the task; a model of what a completed assignment or project should look like)

❑ Monitor rate of presentation of information to student; adapt as necessary

❑ Create paperwork that is concise and neatly organized

❑ Use larger print on paperwork

❑ Include only a few items per page of paperwork

❑ Teach student to use and provide student with supports such as graphic organizers and note taking strategies

(Continued)

Table 3.2 (Continued)

Demonstrating Knowledge of Information

❑ Work with student to determine an appropriate and interesting means for her to demonstrate her knowledge on a topic (e.g., decide if she will make a poster about the topic or take a test)

❑ Develop assignments, projects, and tests that emphasize the quality of information the student can share, rather than the quantity of it

❑ Incorporate use of 3-D objects/manipulatives

❑ Allow student to have a scribe record information

❑ Permit student to tape record information

❑ Let student type, instead of writing by hand

❑ Teach student how to complete a task (e.g., how to take a multiple-choice test)

❑ Give student extended time for completion, if needed

❑ Contemplate using a contract to assist student in understanding the expectations, options, and outcomes associated with a task

❑ Provide student with a model of how a completed assignment, project, or test may look

❑ Consider the sensory needs of student and develop strategies to address them during completion of academic tasks

❑ Provide reinforcement throughout completion of task that is frequent and meaningful to student

❑ Check in with student regarding her progress throughout task

❑ Check in with student regarding her understanding throughout task

❑ Include breaks

❑ Read questions to student

❑ Break a larger task into a series of smaller ones

❑ Highlight important information

❑ Provide positive feedback following completion of task

❑ Create opportunities for repetition of knowledge and/or skill in a variety of environments and with a number of people in an effort to help student generalize and maintain it

❑ Complete on-the-spot modifications as student's needs become apparent

Homework

For students with AS, homework can be a sensitive topic. While homework can be a valuable component of a student's learning process, it does not always serve that function for students with AS. Homework may present two major concerns to students with AS. First, it generally requires that the student write, which can be cognitively and physically challenging. As a result, the student may not be able to demonstrate best what he knows. In addition, many students with AS have to work hard to remain emotionally composed throughout the school day and arrive home exhausted after this daily effort. Therefore, the students need afternoon and evening as a time to relax without demands, as otherwise they may reach their emotional limit for the day, resulting in tantrums, rages, or meltdowns. Further, these students may have additional activities programmed into this time frame, such as attending social skills groups and receiving in-home therapy or support.

Homework should be considered on an individual basis for each child, and any decision should be well thought out and incorporate input from the student, his school team and additional service providers, and his parents. All aspects of homework should be considered during the deci-sion-making process, including (a) how a student will receive information about the homework assignment; (b) how he will complete the assign-ment; and (c) how he will perform all the steps of taking the assignment home, returning it to school, and handing it in. Table 3.3 is a homework checklist that can be used to aid in this decision-making process. In addi-tion, information that will be discussed in the next section, which involves establishing methods of assessment, should be considered in deciding whether or not homework should be used with a student with AS.

SUMMARY

Academic modifications are essential to help students with AS reach their full potential at school. Modifications take into account students' unique strengths, challenges, interests, goals, and learning styles. They can be incorporated into all areas of the curriculum, such as math, science, art, and physical education, and address all aspects of learning from being pre-sented with information, to organizing and learning it, and finally demon-strating knowledge of it. As with the environmental supports discussed in Chapter 2, determining which academic modifications to make for a student with AS is an individualized process that should be based on infor-mation collected from observations, interviews, and assessments involving the student, her teachers and additional service providers, and her parents. Not every strategy discussed here will work for every student with AS, nor is it necessarily true that a student who may benefit from each of these strategies needs all of them. Trial and error will help teacher and student alike learn which modifications provide the most benefit. Consistent moni-toring will then promote the student's continual benefit from these modifi-cations, or indicate that additional fine-tuning of them may be necessary.

Table 3.3   Homework Checklist

1. Decide whether to *(check one)*

    ❑ assign homework

    ❑ provide a homework time during the day

2. Select homework planner that has *(check all that apply)*

    ❑ enough space for the student to write

    ❑ a specific place to write assignments for each class

3. Decide whether *(check one)*

    ❑ teacher(s) will provide student with written homework assignment rather than have student write down homework

    ❑ teacher(s) will prompt the student to write down assignments in planner

4. If the student writes down the assignment *(check all that apply)*

    ❑ teacher(s) will fill in the details student has omitted

    ❑ specific aspects of homework assignments not written by the student will be identified and a system will be taught for handling that portion (i.e., due date)

    ❑ teacher(s) will reinforce student's efforts to write down homework

5. Homework assignments *(check all that apply)*

    ❑ are presented in written form in the same manner and same place every day

    ❑ are specific enough so that parents understand the requirements of the assignment solely from the written information provided

    ❑ include models of assignments whenever possible

6. The home routine for homework completion includes *(check all that apply)*

    ❑ a designated location free from distractions

    ❑ a specific time when homework is completed

    ❑ special considerations for the student (please specify) _____

    ❑ use of textbooks that are kept at home for easy reference

7. A method for clarifying homework is in place that includes *(check all that apply)*

    ❑ a school homework hotline

    ❑ assignments faxed or e-mailed to parents at home

    ❑ a peer buddy who can be called to clarify assignments if needed

8. The plan to monitor completion of and turning in homework includes *(check all that apply)*

    ❑ having a parent sign the homework planner nightly

    ❑ parent-assisted organization of homework assignments in backpack

    ❑ teacher prompt to turn in homework

    ❑ notifying parents weekly of any assignments that have not been turned in

Emotional and Behavioral Supports

4

with Diane Adreon

CASE STUDY: SARAH

Sarah, a first-grade student with AS, receives most of her education in an inclusionary setting. Her general education teacher, with the support of the special educator, has been working on Sarah's transitions from one activity to the next as well as helping her to learn to ask for help. Frequently when Sarah is asked to return to her seat from circle time, she refuses to get up. If her teacher recognizes Sarah's stress level, she can often redirect Sarah to look at her visual schedule and Sarah will immediately calm herself and begin to transition. If, on the other hand, the teacher is not there to prompt Sarah, Sarah will throw herself on the rug and scream and flail for approximately five minutes. Following the tantrum, Sarah will briefly rest before returning to her seat to do her work.

NOTE: Scenario written by Eileen Gorup, Jeanne Holverstott, and Brandy Marie Taylor.

Problems related to innate stress and anxiety are common in children and youth with AS. In fact, this combination has been shown to be one of the most frequently observed co-occurring symptoms in these individuals (Ghaziuddin et al., 1998; Kim, Szatmari, Bryson, Streiner, & Wilson, 2000). They are often triggered or result directly from environmental stressors such as having to face challenging social situations with inadequate social awareness, social understanding, and social problem-solving skills; a sense of loss of control; difficulty in predicting outcomes; an inherent emotional vulnerability; misperception of social events; and a great deal of rigidity in moral judgment that results from a very concrete sense of social justice violations (Church et al., 2000).

The stress experienced by individuals with AS may manifest as withdrawal, reliance on special interests, or inattention and hyperactivity, but it may also trigger aggressive behavior, often seen by educational professionals as tantrums, rage, and "meltdowns" (Myles & Simpson, 2001). This chapter will discuss functional assessment; the cycle of tantrums, rage, and meltdowns; and related interventions as well as stabilization strategies for the student with AS.

FUNCTIONAL ASSESSMENT

Student behaviors are most often associated with a reason or cause. That is, the student is trying to communicate to his teacher that something is wrong, that he is upset or confused, or that he is overwhelmed. Before selecting interventions that might be effective during the rage cycle, it is important to understand why the behavior is occurring. Functional assessment is designed to ask the question, "Why does Mary do _____?" This is the first step in developing effective interventions. Without determining reasons, causes, or conditions under which a behavior occurs, it is unlikely that an intervention will be effective. A functional assessment consists of six steps that are most often carried out by a special educator or school psychologist with assistance from the general educator, speech language pathologist, occupational therapist, or other educational professional. Table 4.1 outlines these steps.

THE CYCLE OF TANTRUMS, RAGE, AND MELTDOWNS

Educators, mental health professionals, and parents often report that children with AS exhibit a sudden onset of aggressive or oppositional behavior. This escalating sequence seems to follow a three-stage cycle (Myles & Southwick, 1999). While non-AS students may recognize and react to the potential for behavioral outbursts early in the cycle, many children and youth with AS endure the entire cycle unaware that they are under stress. That is, while problems of conduct, aggression, and hyperactivity, as well as internalizing problems such as withdrawal, are apparent to their caregivers and teachers, students with AS do not perceive themselves as having problems in these areas (Barnhill, Hagiwara, Myles, Simpson, et al., 2000).

Because of the combination of innate stress and anxiety and the difficulty of children and youth with AS to understand how they feel, it is important that those who work and live with them understand the cycle of tantrums, rage, and meltdowns as well as interventions that can be

Table 4.1   Functional Assessment Steps

Step	Brief Description
Describe student behavior	A student behavior should be described using verbs with information on what it looks like, how often it occurs, and intensity. The teacher who observes, "the student under stress begins to pace rapidly back and forth while whispering" can easily recognize the behavior.
Describe demands of the classroom and other important environments	During this stage, the classroom or other school area is described. This may include an overview of (a) teaching methods, (b) tests, (c) teaching materials, (d) social demands, (e) class management, (f) class structure, and (g) noise level. It is important to describe all parts of the environment that might be causing the behavior.
Collect baseline data	The student should be observed both in the environments where the behavior occurs and where it does not occur.
Complete functional assessment measures and interpret them	Several commercial functional assessment instruments are available to help teachers and parents identify behavior functions (i.e., *Motivation Assessment Scale*, Durand & Crimmins, 1992; *Student-Assisted Functional-Assessment Interview Form*, Kern, Dunlap, Clarke, & Childs, 1994; *Problem Behavior Questionnaire*, Lewis, Scott, & Sugai, 1994). Some special educators may prefer to create their own measures.
Develop a behavioral intervention plan	Once the interpretation has occurred and the cause of the behavior is known, it is time to write a behavioral intervention plan. This plan includes a written description of specific interventions to use with the student to promote behavioral, social, and academic success. In addition, persons who will be responsible for implementation of the plan must be identified.
Collect data to determine effectiveness of the behavioral intervention plan	Data should be collected on the student's behavior. If successful, the plan may need to be continued until the behavior change is permanent. If the intervention is not as effective, it may be necessary to re-examine the reason the behavior occurs and the type of intervention to use, and develop and implement a new behavioral intervention plan.

used to promote self-calming, self-management, and self-awareness as means of preventing or decreasing the severity of behavioral problems.

Tantrums, rage, and meltdowns (terms that are used interchangeably) typically occur in three stages that can be of variable length. These stages are (a) the rumbling stage, (b) the rage stage, and (c) the recovery stage (Albert, 1989; Beck, 1987). Those who work with students with AS should know student stressors and their behavioral indicators. Figure 4.1 overviews the behaviors teachers are likely to see during the cycle. Figure 4.2 highlights interventions for students at the rumbling, rage, and recovery stages. Finally, Figure 4.3 provides an overview of teacher behaviors during the cycle.

Figure 4.1   Student Behavior During the Rage Cycle

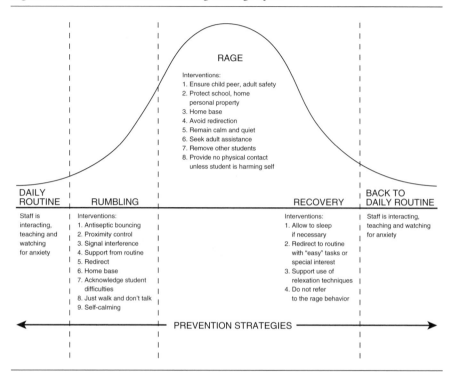

Figure 4.2   Student Interventions During the Rage Cycle

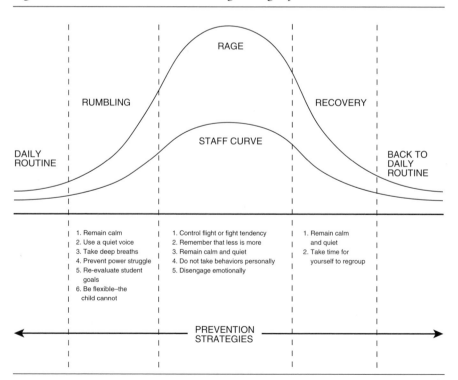

Figure 4.3   Teacher Interventions During the Rage Cycle

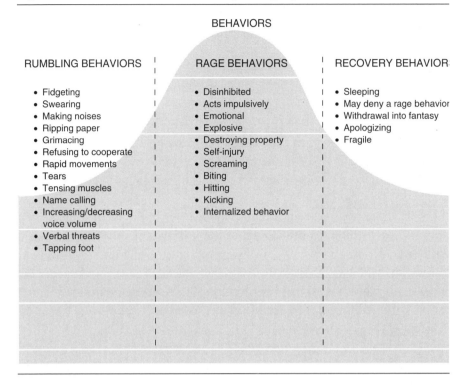

BEHAVIORS

RUMBLING BEHAVIORS	RAGE BEHAVIORS	RECOVERY BEHAVIOR
• Fidgeting	• Disinhibited	• Sleeping
• Swearing	• Acts impulsively	• May deny a rage behavior
• Making noises	• Emotional	• Withdrawal into fantasy
• Ripping paper	• Explosive	• Apologizing
• Grimacing	• Destroying property	• Fragile
• Refusing to cooperate	• Self-injury	
• Rapid movements	• Screaming	
• Tears	• Biting	
• Tensing muscles	• Hitting	
• Name calling	• Kicking	
• Increasing/decreasing	• Internalized behavior	
voice volume		
• Verbal threats		
• Tapping foot		

The Rumbling Stage

The rumbling stage is the initial stage of a tantrum, rage, or meltdown. During this stage, children and youth with AS exhibit specific behavioral changes that may not appear to be directly related to a meltdown and, in fact, may seem minor. For example, they may clear their throats, lower their voices, tense their muscles, tap their feet, or erase their paper until a hole appears. Students may also engage in behaviors that are more obvious, including emotionally or physically withdrawing, or challenging the classroom structure or authority by attempting to engage in a power struggle.

During this stage, it is imperative that an adult intervene without becoming part of the struggle. Interventions that occur during this stage include: antiseptic bouncing, proximity control, signal interference, support from routine (Long, Morse, & Newman, 1976), redirecting, home base, acknowledging student difficulties, just walk and don't talk, and self-calming. All of these strategies can be effective in stopping the cycle of tantrums, rage, and meltdowns, and they are invaluable in that they can help the child regain control with minimal adult support (Myles & Southwick, 1999). These strategies share the following commonalities: (a) they limit adult verbalization, (b) they have student choice options, and (c) they can be used flexibly to meet student needs.

At this stage, the teacher needs to be flexible as the student cannot. The strategies do not, however, replace stabilization strategies. Interventions used during the rage cycle can be thought of as band-aids that allow the student and adults to survive the cycle. When the student is in the rumbling stage, the teacher needs to evaluate his or her goals for the student. For example, Mack began to exhibit rumbling-stage behaviors when he was half finished with his math page. His teacher, when planning which strategy to use, reminded himself that his primary goal was to help Mack learn to control his behavior. So he selected antiseptic bouncing, realizing that completing the math assignment was of secondary importance to helping Mack control his behavior.

Antiseptic Bouncing. Antiseptic bouncing involves removing a student, in a nonpunitive fashion, from the environment in which she is experiencing difficulty. At school, this may involve sending the child on an errand. At home, the child may be asked to retrieve an object for a parent. During this time, the student has an opportunity to regain a sense of calm. When she returns, the problem has typically diminished in magnitude, and the adult is on hand for support, if needed.

Proximity Control. Rather than calling attention to behavior in a more demonstrative way, using proximity control the teacher moves near the student who is engaged in the target behavior. Something as simple as standing next to a child is often calming and can easily be accomplished without interrupting an ongoing activity. For example, the teacher who circulates through the classroom during a lesson is using proximity control.

Signal Interference. When the child with AS begins to exhibit a behavior that occurs just prior to a tantrum, rage, or meltdown, such as clearing the throat or pacing, the teacher can use a nonverbal signal to let the student know that she is aware of the situation. For example, the teacher can place herself in a position where she can maintain eye contact with the student. Or an agreed-upon "secret signal," such as tapping on a desk, may be used to alert the child that he is under stress. Signal interference may be followed by an in-seat destressor, such as squeezing a stress ball that has been prescribed by an occupational therapist. Often this strategy precedes antiseptic bouncing.

Support from Routine. Displaying a chart or visual schedule of expectations and events can provide security to children and youth with AS who typically need predictability. This technique can also be used as advance preparation for a change in routine. Informing students of schedule changes can prevent anxiety and reduce the likelihood of tantrums, rage, and meltdowns. For example, the student who is signaling frustration by tapping his foot may be directed to his schedule to remind him that after he completes two more problems he gets to work on a topic of special interest with a peer.

Redirecting. Redirecting involves helping the student to focus on something other than the task or activity that appears to be upsetting the student. One type of redirection that often works well when the source of the behavior is a lack of understanding is telling the child that he can cartoon the situation with you in order to figure out what to do (see Chapter 5). Sometimes cartooning can be briefly postponed. At other times, the student may need to cartoon immediately. Redirection can also involve the adult introducing a discussion on the child's special interest, which may serve as a calming agent for the child.

Home Base. As mentioned earlier, home base is a place in the school where an individual can escape stress. The home base should be quiet, with few visual or activity distractions, and activities should be selected carefully to ensure that they are calming rather than alerting. In school, resource rooms or counselors' offices can serve as a home base. The structure of the room supercedes its location. Regardless of its location, it is essential that the home base be viewed as a positive environment. Home base is not time out or an escape from classroom tasks or chores. The student takes class work to home base, which is completed after a brief respite (Myles & Simpson, 2002).

Home base may be used at times other than during the rumbling stage. For example, at the beginning of the day, a home base can be used to preview the day's schedule, introduce changes in the typical routine, ensure that the student's materials are organized, or prime for specific subjects. At other times, it can be used to help the student gain control after a meltdown (see recovery stage).

Acknowledging Student Difficulties. This technique is effective when the student is in the midst of the rumbling stage because of a difficult task and the parent or educator thinks that the student can complete the activity with support. The parent or teacher offers a brief acknowledgment that supports the verbalizations of the child and helps her complete her task. For example, when working on a math problem the student begins to say, "This is too hard." Knowing the student is capable of completing the problem, the teacher refocuses the student's attention by saying, "Yes, the problem is difficult. Let's start with number one." This brief direction and support may prevent the student from moving past the rumbling stage.

Just Walk and Don't Talk. The adult using this technique merely walks with the student without talking. Silence on the part of the adult is important because a child with AS in the rumbling stage will likely react emotively to any statement, misinterpreting it or rephrasing it beyond recognition. On this walk, the child can say whatever she wishes without fear of discipline or logical argument. In the meantime, the adult should be calm, show as little reaction as possible, and never be confrontational (Myles & Southwick, 1999; Ottinger, 2003).

Self-Calming. Even though children and adolescents do not engage in the tantrums, rage, and meltdowns purposefully, they need strategies to stop the cycle during its early stages. The self-relaxation strategy developed by Buron (2003) for students with autism spectrum disorders is particularly applicable. Her routine, entitled the "relaxed body," includes a series of flexible steps that can be matched to student needs. For 4-year-old Nicholas, the strategy included:

1. Take three long breaths.

2. Stretch your arms up over your head, down, and up again.

3. Rub your hands together and count to 3.

4. Rub your thighs and count to 3.

5. Take another long breath.

Dunn's (2000) intervention is intended to help children with AS and related disabilities by teaching them to rate their behavior on a 5-point scale, with a rating of 1 meaning little or no stress and a rating of 5 indicating that stress may result in a meltdown (see Chapter 5).

When selecting an intervention during the rumbling stage, it is important to know the student well, as the wrong technique can escalate rather than de-escalate a behavior problem. Further, while interventions at this stage do not require extensive time, it is advisable that adults understand the events that precipitate the target behaviors so that they can (a) be ready to intervene early or (b) teach children and youth strategies to maintain behavioral control during these times.

Just as it is important to understand interventions that may diffuse a crisis, it is imperative that adults know which behaviors are likely to escalate the child from the rumbling to the rage stage. Finally, interventions at this stage are merely palliative. That is, they do not teach students to recognize their frustration or provide a means of handling it.

Teacher Behaviors During the Rumbling Stage

While attention is often paid to student behaviors and interventions, few have discussed the staff curve that occurs during a student's rage cycle. As children escalate, adults who have not worked extensively with children with AS are also prone to escalate. During the rumbling cycle, educational professionals must remain calm and project calmness by using a quiet voice and taking deep breaths. Minimized verbalizations decrease the likelihood that a power struggle will ensue. This is also the ideal time to re-evaluate the student's goals. During the rumbling stage, a primary focus should be preventing the occurrence of the rage stage. This may mean leaving an assignment unfinished. The teacher must be flexible as the student experiencing rumbling behaviors cannot.

The Rage Stage

If behavior is not diffused during the rumbling stage, the child or adolescent may move to the rage stage. At this point, the student is disinhibited and acts impulsively, emotionally, and sometimes explosively. These behaviors may be externalized (i.e., screaming, biting, hitting, kicking, destroying property or self-injury) or internalized (i.e., withdrawal). Meltdowns are not purposeful, and once the rage stage begins, it most often must run its course.

During this stage, emphasis should be placed on child, peer, and adult safety as well as protection of school or personal property. One method of coping with a tantrum, rage, or meltdown is to get the child to home base. This is possible only if you can support the child's move to home base without using physical restraint. In general, avoid redirection as a strategy at this stage. It only escalates behavior and causes confusion as the child is unlikely to be able to process the teacher commands that he hears. Thus, it is important that the teacher remains calm and quiet, and projects that appearance.

Of importance here is helping the individual with AS regain control and preserve dignity. To that end, adults should have developed plans for (a) obtaining assistance from other educators such as a crisis teacher or principal, or (b) removing other students from the area, or (c) providing therapeutic restraint, if necessary. Generally, restraint should be used only if the child is harming himself.

Teacher Behaviors During the Rage Stage

As student anxiety and related behaviors increase, so does teacher anxiety. Buron (personal communication, January 15, 2004) cautions teachers working with students in crisis to "Be quiet, calm, and confident. This is the peak of adult anxiety, too. The instinct is fight or flight, but neither is possible." During this stage, it is important to understand the concept that "less is more." The teacher should remain quiet and calm without taking any student rage behavior personally. Disengaging emotionally during the student's cycle is necessary so that the teacher does not escalate her behavior.

The Recovery Stage

Following a meltdown, the child with AS may become apologetic and often cannot fully remember what occurred during the rage stage. Some may become sullen, withdraw, or deny that inappropriate behavior occurred, while others are so physically exhausted that they need to sleep.

It is imperative that interventions are implemented at a time when the student can accept them and in a manner the student can understand and accept. Otherwise, the intervention may simply resume the cycle in a more accelerated pattern leading more quickly to the rage stage. During the recovery stage, children are often not ready to learn. Thus, it is important that adults work with them to help them to once again become a part of the routine. This is often best accomplished by directing the youth to a highly motivating task that can be easily completed, such as an activity related to a special interest. Some students may need to engage in self-relaxation techniques (see Buron, 2003) or engage in sensory activities to meet this end. The teacher should not refer to the rage behaviors at this time as the student is not ready to process or learn new skills that can prevent future meltdowns.

Teacher Behaviors During the Recovery Stage

During this stage, as in the others, the teacher must remain calm and quiet. Once the child has been redirected to a structured activity, it is important that the teacher take time for herself to regroup. Regrouping may include leaving the class briefly, taking deep breaths, filing, or engaging in another brief activity that is calming.

STABILIZATION

Children and youth with AS experience stress and anxiety that has been linked to difficulties in adapting to change, predicting what will happen next, understanding the social interactions and intentions of others, depression, and so forth (Barnhill, 2001; Myles & Southwick, 1999). When students have difficulty adapting to their environment, they may begin a downward spiral. When this cycle begins, the priority must be to stabilize them. "Stabilization" refers to the process of creating an environment that assists the individual in becoming more stable and therefore function better (Myles & Adreon, 2001).

Short-Term Interventions

Stabilization strategies may be required because of short- or long-term events. If a child experiences several changes or disappointments within a short period of time, she may become less stable or more vulnerable to a tantrum, rage, or meltdown. To become more stable, the student needs the environment adapted. Adaptations are often minor, and may include antiseptic bouncing, support from routine, reassurance, proximity control, "just walk and don't talk," or home base. For example, when Roberto came into the cafeteria he saw that the tables were not in their usual place; they were moved to the far side of the room. He got into the lunch line and found that the cafeteria was out of pizza, the food he ate almost every day. Roberto chose a hot dog instead. Mr. Smith, the assistant principal, monitors Roberto's lunch period and knows him well. He noticed that two of Roberto's peers who have teased him in the past sat down at his table. As a result, he walked over to Roberto's table frequently during the lunch period, checking to make sure that Roberto was okay and listening to gain a sense of the peer interactions. Mr. Smith also made a point to ask Roberto about recently televised political debates because that is one of Roberto's special interests. In addition, when Roberto finished, Mr. Smith gave him a job to do—taking a note to the office—that allowed him to leave the lunchroom area.

In this instance, Roberto experienced three minor stressors (rearrangement of the lunchroom, no pizza, and exposure to peers with whom he had problems). Mr. Smith reacted to the situation by making sure that Roberto was safe from teasing, by focusing on one of his favorite topics (political debates), and by asking Roberto to take a note to the office, thereby giving him an opportunity to leave the cafeteria (antiseptic bouncing).

Long-Term Interventions

Stabilization for individuals who have had long-term problems is different. The longer the student has been in a downward spiral, the more difficult it is to reverse the trend. Martha is repeating the ninth grade in a general education setting. Her teachers report that she seems withdrawn and depressed and is producing no work. This was true last year, too. Even when the teacher prompts her to do her work, Martha says she cannot or puts her head down on her desk and sleeps. Her behavioral program consists of a token economy system that is tallied weekly. Frequently, Martha does not earn enough tokens for a reward. When her case manager suggested that the curriculum needed further adaptation around Martha's interests, staff emphasized that she had to participate in the regular curriculum since she is on the standard diploma track.

Changing Martha's situation required a significant cognitive shift on the part of the school team serving her. Once a student has "shut down," she is incapable of coping with many typical school demands. It does not matter that the student has an average or above-average IQ. That, in and of itself, does not mean that the student is in an emotional state that allows her to conform to environmental demands. It is essential that the school team (including parents) recognize the fragile emotional state of the student with AS and adapt the environment to meet her needs.

Martha was eventually moved to a resource room setting where a teacher could work with her one-on-one. Further, curricular demands were modified drastically, all instruction focused around her special interest—electromagnetism—and assignments contained tasks that Martha had previously mastered. The daily schedule was structured and consistent, and visual supports were used to help Martha keep track of her day. Finally, stressors such as tests and handwriting were removed. Emphasis was placed on motivating Martha to learn, increase self-esteem, and to make her feel safe and comfortable. In addition, her parents, deciding that therapy would be beneficial, found a therapist who understood AS. The therapist bonded with Martha and helped her develop a better self-esteem and a sense of trust toward her teachers.

As Martha's emotional state began to improve, her teacher and therapist worked on helping Martha recognize her own indicators of stress and seek assistance. Six months later, Martha was ready to gradually transition back into general education. Her school team, deciding to move her into one class at a time, helped her to transition into science, an area of strength and motivation.

Five Steps to Help Stabilize a Student With ASD

The following five steps can help students who require stabilization:

1. Gather information from several sources to assess the student's emotional state. Students with AS require continuous monitoring of their emotional status. Often teachers and parents miss the signs that signal the beginning of a crisis. This is due, in part, to the communication deficits of students with AS. That is, they are often ineffective at recognizing in

themselves and conveying anxiety, frustration, anger, or depression until these emotions have reached crisis proportions. Therefore, educators and parents must become skilled at recognizing the initial behavioral signs of stress and anxiety. Melinda's teachers and parents know that when she starts to pace back and forth Melinda is anxious. Sam runs his hand through his hair when he encounters too much stress. Min begins to rock back and forth when he experiences difficulty.

A second indicator of declining emotional status is deterioration in academic, social, or behavior functioning at school or home. It is important to keep in mind that academic decline includes a student with AS who usually gets an "A" in science and now is getting a "C."

It is common for schools to report that the student is doing fine during the school day (no behavioral outbursts, good attention to task, appropriate social skills), whereas the parent reports that the student falls apart at home (uncontrollable tantrums, verbal outbursts, aggression against siblings) (Myles & Southwick, 1999). This type of behavior at home signals that stressors may exist in school or at home.

2. Determine the stressors that exist in the environment. It is important to determine whether any changes have occurred at school or home that might have caused or contributed to the downward spiral. For example:

- Has the student had to cope with a substitute teacher?
- Has the regular schedule been interrupted (i.e., assemblies, testing)?
- Does the student have a long-term assignment to do with no idea of how to begin?
- Has the structure in specific classes been changed (i.e. from individual work to cooperative groups)?
- Has the student been exposed to teasing or bullying?
- Has the student reported difficulties in working with a particular student?
- Has increased emphasis been placed on getting good grades?

3. Decrease the stressors by modifying the requirements for disliked or difficult tasks and temporarily eliminating any emphasis on teaching new skills. To stabilize the school environment and stop the escalating crisis, we must increase supports immediately and reduce stressors. It is imperative that school personnel and parents identify specific situations that may routinely lead to tantrums, rage, and meltdowns (Green, 1998).

If the difficulty experienced in one area is of considerable magnitude, or if the student is experiencing difficulty in a number of areas, it is important that interventions be implemented on multiple levels concurrently. Thus, when supports are increased tenfold, the student is more likely to bounce back than if supports are increased individually over several weeks or months. It is important for the child or adolescent to receive some respite from stressors. For example, if a major stressor for the student is coping with the long-term substitute language arts teacher, the school team (including the parents) may decide that the language arts requirements may be modified for the next long-term assignment. Or they may decide that the student can receive language arts instruction in a resource room.

When the student is in a fragile emotional state, school personnel and parents must recognize the necessity of temporarily lowering their expectations. For example, the student may need to know how to write essays when she attends college, but that does not mean that in a crisis state she must practice writing every day. The more fragile the emotional state, the more crucial it is that the stressors be alleviated.

While reducing stressors, it may be important at the same time to provide more opportunities for the student with AS to engage in activities of high interest or activities that emphasize strengths. Omar derives considerable self-esteem from the fact that many teachers call on him to assist with computer problems. When Omar began having meltdowns during physical education (PE) class, a variety of interventions were put in place. When none of them proved successful, the school team decided to waive the PE requirement and build additional computer technical assistance opportunities into Omar's daily schedule.

4.   Make the environment more predictable and increase the use of home base. The student's many environments should be reanalyzed to ensure a high level of consistency and to ascertain that the student knows the routine in each class. Priming may need to be used more frequently. In addition, the student may need to have written into her schedule home base periods that occur both prior to and following a class that is especially difficult. For example, Jerry's homeroom teacher noticed that he is often on edge when he arrives at school. Knowing his interest in drawing cartoon figures, the teacher allowed him to come to the classroom as soon as his bus arrives, thus allowing him 15 to 20 minutes to draw and get himself ready to face the school day.

5.   Balance stressors and learning. As the student with AS becomes more stable, it is possible to gradually increase regular demands. The key to success is continually monitoring the student's emotional status and maintaining supports. As demands are increased, careful assessment must determine whether the individual has the skill(s) to perform the

increased tasks. If not, a plan must be developed to teach the skills. For some students, instruction in these skills should occur in a structured classroom-type setting. Others may benefit from planned moments of instruction, that is, providing a brief explanation or coaching when a social error happens. However, care should be taken that this instruction is not a stressor in itself. Jerry's school created a pull-out social skills group for him, but after a while, his teachers noticed that he began to talk about the group a day or two before it was scheduled. In addition, they reported an increase in Jerry's identified anxiety behaviors (humming, rubbing his eyes, and repeated questioning) the day before the group was to meet. Noting his agitation, Jerry's parents and school team decided that he would benefit more from embedded instruction in his general education classroom than continued participation in the pull-out social skills group.

When a student is not stable, it is essential that the school team identify contributing factors and devise comprehensive strategies to turn the situation around for the child or youth with AS. The key to success involves continually monitoring the individual's emotional state and maintaining the level of supports needed to make school a successful experience.

SUMMARY

Children and youth with AS generally do not want to engage in tantrums, rage, and meltdowns. Rather, the rage cycle is the only way they know of expressing stress and coping with problems and a host of other emotions. Most want to learn methods to manage their behavior, including calming themselves in the face of problems and increasing self-awareness of their emotions.

The best intervention for tantrums, rage, and meltdowns is prevention. Prevention occurs best as a multifaceted approach, depending on why the student with AS is experiencing meltdowns. If the student is experiencing behavior problems because of social challenges, he or she needs social skills support in the hidden curriculum or other social mores using instructional, interpretive, and coaching strategies that help students understand the world around them as well as themselves (see Chapter 5 for a discussion of social supports). If, on the other hand, the student with AS is having meltdowns because of environmental or academic factors, then the strategies discussed in Chapters 2, 3, and 6 can be effective in preventing behavioral challenges.

Social Skills Supports

5

CASE STUDY: TED

Ted, a 13-year-old with AS who has always had difficulty with social situations, observed that many students at his middle school cursed. Noticing that the colorful words appeared to cause laughter, he concluded that cursing would impress his peers—something that he was eager to do. Consequently, during the passing period between second and third hour he walked up to a boy he knew and began to talk to him, infusing curse words into his conversation. The boy stared at Ted but said nothing. Ted was startled when the principal interrupted his conversation and ordered him to the office.

The first criterion listed in the DSM IV-TR (APA, 2000) for a diagnosis of AS is an impairment in social interaction. In fact, many believe that this characteristic is the one that is most distinctive of individuals with AS (Broderick, Caswell, Gregor, Marzolini, & Wilson, 2002; Church et al., 2000). Researchers and practitioners have discussed the negative impact of not having appropriate social skills, ranging from the inability to develop and maintain friendships to being ridiculed by peers to not being able to keep a job due to a lack of understanding of workplace culture and relationships between supervisors and colleagues (Baron-Cohen, O'Riordan, Stone, Jones, & Plaisted, 1999; Engstrom, Ekstrom, & Emilsson, 2003).

Social skills is a complex human behavior. Although somewhat rule governed, the rules vary across location, situations, people, age, and culture, making it difficult to acquire and generalize skills. Greeting is one example of a social skill that is assumed to be simple. However, further analysis shows this skill is extremely complex. How a child greets a friend in the classroom differs from the type of greeting he would use if the two met at a local restaurant. The greeting used the first time the child sees a friend differs from the greeting used when they see each other later in the day. Further, words and actions for greetings differ depending on whether

75

the child is greeting a teacher or a peer. Thus, greetings are complex, as are most other social skills.

Particularly in schools, certain social supports appear essential, including (a) understanding unwritten social rules, (b) knowing how to make friends, (c) having skills to support social interaction, (d) having someone who can explain or interpret social situations that the student with AS did not understand or that did not occur as planned, and (e) understanding how sensory needs can impact interactions.

HIDDEN CURRICULUM

The hidden curriculum refers to the set of rules that everyone in the school knows, but that no one has been directly taught (Bieber, 1994). Wide ranging, the hidden curriculum includes subtle elements such as how to dress, how to act, what to do and what not to do and when, who to talk to, who to ignore, and so on. It also includes knowing (a) teacher expectations, (b) teacher-pleasing behaviors, (c) students who potentially make good friends versus individuals who are likely to get you in trouble, (d) behaviors that attract positive attention from teachers and peers, and (e) behaviors that are considered negative or inappropriate by teachers and peers (Myles & Simpson, 2001).

The hidden curriculum is known by most people, yet taken for granted. Every school and, indeed, every society has a hidden curriculum. This unspoken curriculum is challenging for individuals with AS because they do not learn social skills and related items incidentally.

It is imperative that the child or youth with AS understand her teachers' personalities and expectations. Almost all students know their teachers by the end of the first week at school. For example, they know which teachers they can joke with, which teachers will not tolerate certain comments, which teachers allow late assignments, and which teachers do not grade quizzes closely. Simply by being in class and observing human nature, most youths understand their teachers' quirks, preferences, and unspoken rules.

Everyone knows that Mrs. Miller allows students to whisper in class as long as they get their work done, whereas Mrs. Cook does not tolerate any level of noise in her class. Similarly, everyone knows that Mr. Hudson, the assistant principal, is a stickler for following the rules, so no one curses or even slouches in his presence. Everyone also knows that the really tough guys (the ones who harass smaller and weaker students) hang out behind the slide, just out of teacher view. Everyone knows these things—except the student with AS.

Outside of school, the hidden curriculum is a greater enigma for students with AS. For example, what is the hidden curriculum for taking rides from or talking to strangers? The bus driver is a stranger, but it is permissible to accept a ride from her. It is not okay to ride with the stranger who pulls up to the curb and stops. The cashier at the grocery store is a stranger, but it is acceptable to make small talk with her. It is not acceptable to divulge personal information to someone who is standing in the produce section. It is suitable to accept candy from the distributor who is giving free samples at a local toy store, yet it is not prudent to take candy from a stranger standing on the street corner.

Although invaluable, this type of survival information is usually not available to individuals with AS, and the only manner in which they will learn it is through direct instruction. Someone, usually a person with whom the student has rapport, must instruct the student on the hidden curriculum. Knowing the hidden curriculum is essential for children and youth with AS, as it can keep them out of trouble and help them make friends (Myles & Simpson, 2003). Some hidden curriculum items that may merit consideration:

- Place the cap back on any pen or marker that you have been using.
- Adjust your voice level to an "inside" voice in the classroom.
- Raise your hand to get your teacher's attention.
- Raise your hand when the teacher pauses, instead of when he or she is in the middle of explaining something.
- It's okay to make a mistake—use white-out or an eraser.
- If someone is doing something in class that is bothering you or making you uncomfortable, ask them to please stop and tell them why it bothers you.
- Always keep your hands and feet to yourself.
- Be willing to try new activities and skills.
- When saying the Pledge of Allegiance or singing the Star Spangled Banner, refrain from talking or laughing.
- Walk inside the classroom.
- While working, keep your eyes on your own paper.
- During silent reading, read in your mind, not out loud.
- Be on time to class.
- Make eye contact with the teacher to let him or her know you are listening.
- Limit yourself to five questions during a subject in school. If you continue to ask questions, it may bother the other students and the teacher.
- When you are assigned to a group, stay with that group until the teacher changes it.
- Do not draw violent scenes in school.

- In middle school, each teacher will have different rules. It is important to know the rules for each teacher and it will do no good to say that it is not fair.
- When the teacher is giving a lesson, it is time to listen. Talking about topics that you are interested in can take place at a later time.
- If you have a guest speaker, do not interrupt his or her speech. Ask questions at the end of the speech.
- Most teachers do not allow gum in school. Chew gum after school.
- Teachers give students transition statements—learn what your teacher uses so you can be ready to go to the next subject or activity. Some teachers may tell you that you will be leaving in 5 minutes. That may mean 2 minutes or 10 minutes. You will know that you are leaving soon.
- If you pass notes in class to a friend, do it discreetly so the teacher does not catch you.
- You will probably be teased if someone sees you tasting glue at school.
- Keep personal information about your family to yourself during school.
- Even if other students write in their textbooks or on their desks, use a piece of paper instead so you won't get in trouble.
- When it is time to clean up, it does not have to be perfect. The janitor will come in after school to vacuum and do the final clean-up.
- When standing in line, make sure there is enough space for one or two people between you and the person in front of you.
- If a teacher tells another student to stop talking, it is a good idea for you to also stop talking since the teacher has already expressed disapproval of talking.
- If you get in trouble once, it does not mean that your entire day is ruined.
- When someone else is getting in trouble, it is not the time to ask questions or show the teacher something.
- If the teacher crosses her arms and clears her throat, she either wants the class to be quiet or to look up and get ready to listen to a direction.
- If your teacher gives you a warning about behavior and you continue the behavior you will probably get in trouble. If you stop the behavior immediately after the warning, you will probably not get into trouble.

From *Asperger Syndrome and the Hidden Curriculum: Practical Solutions for Understanding Unwritten Rules,* by B. S. Myles and M. Trautman (2004). Reprinted with permission from Autism Asperger Publishing Company, Shawnee Mission, KS.

SOCIAL STRATEGIES

A multifaceted approach to social skills is necessary to assist children and youth with AS to understand how to use and interpret social skills in the

Table 5.1   Overview of Social Supports

Area	Strategy	Developed By		Used By	
		Gen.	Spec.	Gen.	Spec.
Instruction					
	Scope and sequence	X	X	X	X
	Direct instruction		X	X	X
	Social narratives	X	X	X	X
	Power Card strategy		X	X	X
	Acting lessons		X		X
	Self-esteem building		X	X	X
	Self-awareness		X	X	X
	Circle of friends		X	X	X
Interpretation					
	Cartooning		X		X
	Social autopsies		X	X	X
	SOCCSS		X		X
	Sensory awareness	X	X		X
Coaching					
	Feeding the language	X	X	X	X
	Conversation starters	X	X	X	X
	Video self-modeling		X		X

school, home, and community. This approach includes (a) instruction, (b) interpretation, and (c) coaching. *Instruction* refers to providing direct assistance to children and youth with AS in skill provision. *Interpretation* is recognizing that, no matter how well-developed the instructional program for the person with AS, situations will arise that the person does not understand. As a result, someone in the person's environment must assume the role of interpreter. These strategies help students learn to self-monitor their behavior and social skills as well as make good decisions. The third element, *coaching*, cues the students with AS to use the skills they have learned during instruction and interpretation. Table 5.1 provides an overview of the strategies that can be used during instruction, interpretation, and coaching and indicates whether a general or special educator is most likely to develop and implement the strategy.

Instruction

Students with AS demonstrate many social deficits and differences that require instruction to ensure they acquire the skills that facilitate self-awareness, self-calming, and self-management. Most often, without a planned instructional sequence these students do not learn many of the skills that we take for granted. Considerations for instruction include (a) scope and sequence, (b) direct instruction, (c) social narratives, (d) the Power Card strategy, (e) acting lessons, (f) self-esteem building, (g) self-awareness, and (h) Circle of Friends.

Scope and Sequence

Because children and youth with AS exhibit an uneven profile of social skills, it is important to understand the sequence in which these skills develop. Without an understanding of scope and sequence, it is possible to overlook that a child may be missing an important prerequisite skill that might make a more advanced skill rote-based instead of a usable asset. For example, if a student does not understand that tone of voice communicates a message, teaching the more advanced skill of using a respectful tone of voice to teachers may have little or no meaning. If the student learns by rote to use that tone of voice, it will likely not generalize.

Several scopes and sequences exist that include skills that specifically support self-awareness, self-calming, and self-management. For example, Baker (2003) provides an extensive list of skills in hierarchical order in his book *Social Skills Training for Children and Adolescents with Asperger Syndrome and Social Communication Problems.* His scope and sequence includes both communication skills and emotion management skills. Specifically, communication skills cover (a) conversational skills, (b) cooperative play skills, and (c) friendship management. Emotion management skills include (a) self-regulation, (b) empathy, and (c) conflict management. This scope and sequence has been used successfully in Baker's clinical practice for over 20 years.

Direct Instruction

Direct instruction refers to teaching social skills in a purposeful and meaningful way, similar to the way in which teachers teach reading, math, or other academic skills. The following direct instructional sequence facilitates learning of social skills: (a) rationale, (b) presentation, (c) modeling, (d) verification, (e) evaluation, and (f) generalization.

For instruction to be effective, students with AS often need to understand the *rationale*—how or why concepts required for mastery are relevant. Thus, the rationale for a social skill should include (a) why the information is useful, (b) how the student can use the information, and (c) where it fits in with the knowledge the student already possesses. Presenting this information using a visual support will help the youth with AS understand what she is going to learn, the activities she will complete to practice the skill, and the length of time she will spend in social skills instruction.

The *presentation* should be active. Individuals with AS not only need to listen to and view content, but also to respond to questions, share their observations, and receive corrective feedback. Information must be presented using both visual and auditory formats.

During *modeling*, the student is shown what to do. One common mistake must be avoided: we often tell students what *not* to do without providing the alternative—what they are supposed to do. Modeling should occur frequently, with the context for its use clearly delineated. We cannot infer that the student understands a specific concept or format just because it has been presented before.

Anything merely implied will likely not be understood by the student. As a result, *verification* must occur throughout the lesson. That is, the teacher must closely monitor the student's understanding of what is being taught and his emotional state. Because students with AS often have a flat, even seemingly negative affect, it is difficult to tell when they understand a concept or are confused. The teacher must work with the student to understand how he communicates understanding.

Following verification, evaluation of social skill acquisition should occur. A variety of methods should be employed to assess student understanding and use of the skill. For example, students should self-evaluate their skill performance and set goals for generalization and skill maintenance. Teachers should similarly ensure that assessment of skills occurs in the natural environment.

Finally, programming for generalization should be a part of every lesson through opportunities for students to use newly acquired social skills during the school day and in a variety of settings (i.e., science class, music). The student should also be observed in less structured settings, such as lunch and recess, to determine whether a given skill has truly been generalized. Assistance from parents is invaluable to ensure generalization. Specifically, they can set up or observe home- and community-based events in which the student is expected to use a given skill.

Direct instruction lessons can be drawn from traditional or nontraditional curricula. Traditional curricula such as McAfee's (2002) *Navigating the Social World: A Curriculum for Individuals with Asperger's Syndrome, High Functioning Autism, and Related Disorders*; Baker's (2003) *Social Skills Training for Children and Adolescents with Asperger Syndrome and Social Communication Problems*; or Gutstein and Sheely's (2002) *Relationship Development Intervention with Children and Adolescents and Adults: Social and Emotional Development Activities for Asperger Syndrome, Autism, PDD, and NLD* are excellent sources. Nontraditional curricula such as *Bringing Up Parents: The Teenager's Handbook* (Packer, 1992); *How Rude! The Teenager's*

Guide to Manners, Proper Behavior, and Not Grossing People Out (Packer, 1997); and the American Girls Series by the Pleasant Company are excellent resources.

Social Narratives

Social narratives provide support and instruction for children and adolescents with AS who engage in interactions by describing social cues and appropriate responses to social behavior and teaching new social skills. Written by educators at the child's instructional level, and often using pictures or photographs to confirm content, social narratives can promote self-awareness, self-calming, and self-management. Minimal guidelines exist for creating social narratives other than to ensure that the content matches student needs and takes student perspective into account (Myles, Trautman, & Schelvan, 2004). There are two types of social narratives: Social Stories and scripts. The following are guidelines for writing social narratives:

1. Identify a social situation for intervention. The social narrative author should select a social behavior to be changed, preferably one whose improvement can result in positive social interactions, a safer environment, additional social learning opportunities, or all three.

2. Define target behavior for data collection. It is necessary to clearly define the behavior on which data will be collected. The behavior should be defined in such a way that the student and everyone who will be collecting data understands it.

3. Collect baseline data on the target behavior. Collecting data over an extended period allows the educator to determine a trend. Baseline data collection can last from three to five days or longer.

4. Write a social narrative using language at the child's level. Consider whether to use first person (I) or third person (you) language. Social narratives should be written in accordance with the student's comprehension skills, with vocabulary and print size individualized for each student. The author must decide whether the social narrative would be more effective if it is written with "I" statements (e.g., I need to remember to . . .) or "you" statements (e.g., You need to remember that . . .). In addition, the narrative can be constructed using present or future tense (to describe a situation as it occurs or to anticipate an upcoming event, respectively).

5. Choose the number of sentences per page according to the student's functioning level. Presentation of the social narrative must

match the student's functioning level. For some students, one to three sentences per page is adequate. Each sentence allows the student to focus on and process a specific concept. For others, more than one sentence per page may result in an overload of information such that the student does not comprehend the information.

6. Use photographs, hand-drawn pictures, or pictorial icons. Pictures, such as photographs, hand-drawn pictures, or computer-generated icons, may enhance student understanding of appropriate behavior, especially with students who lack or who have emerging reading skills.

7. Read the social narrative to the student and model the desired behavior. Reading the social narrative and modeling related behaviors as needed should become a consistent part of the student's daily schedule. The student who is able to read independently may read the narrative to peers or adults so that all have a similar understanding of the targeted situation and appropriate behaviors.

8. Collect intervention data. The author should collect data using the procedures described for collecting and analyzing baseline data.

9. Review the findings and the narrative. If the student does not respond with the desired behavior after approximately two weeks from the introduction of the social narrative, the author should review the narrative and its implementation procedures. It is recommended that if program alterations are made, only one variable should be changed at a time (e.g., change only the content of the story, rather than simultaneously changing the time the story is read and the person who reads it). By changing only one factor at a time, the educator can determine the factor or factors that best facilitate a student's learning.

10. Program for maintenance and generalization. After a behavior change has become consistent, the educator may want to fade use of the social narrative. Fading may be accomplished by extending the time between readings or having students be responsible for reading the story themselves. In some cases, the social narrative is not faded. This decision should be made on a case-by-case basis.

Social Stories^{TM}. The most often used social narrative is Social Stories™ (Gray, 1995, 2000; Gray & Gerand, 1993). Gray created Social Stories™ to describe social situations specific to individuals and circumstances, but cautions that they should not be used to change behavior (Gray, 2000). Gray's (2000) guidelines for Social Story development include (a) picturing the goal, (b) gathering information, (c) tailoring the text, and (d) teaching with the title. The following is a Social Story about sharing:

Sometimes at school, other children want to play with the toys I have or read the books I am reading. They ask me to share these things because they like them, too.

When they ask me to share, I have many choices. I can tell them to ask the teacher to help us share fairly. I can also say, "okay" and give them what they want. Another thing I can do is say, "I am playing with this right now, but you can have it when I'm done."

When I growl at other children instead of using my choices, the other kids get mad or laugh at me. This makes me feel mad. Sometimes the teacher hears me growl and this makes her upset. Then I get in trouble.

I don't want to get mad or in trouble, so I will use my choices when children want me to share.

Scripts. Scripts are written sentences or paragraphs or videotaped scenarios that individuals with AS can memorize and use in social situations (Kamps, Kravits, & Ross, 2002). The scripts are memorized and practiced with an adult or other peers, then used in real-life situations. This type of coaching is used for children with AS who have difficulty generating novel language when under stress, but have excellent rote memories. Care should be taken that scripts include "child- or adolescent-friendly language." That is, common jargon should be incorporated as well as the informal language style evidenced by peers. Scripts do not work in every situation as they may make a child or adolescent sound over-rehearsed or robotic. They are best used with model peers who understand the child, her characteristics, and the purpose of scripts. The following is a script developed for Jonah by Jennifer Savner Levinson about appropriate words to use with adults and peers:

Kids use different words when they talk with adults than when they talk with their friends. It is important to know this difference.

Here are some words that can be said to adults:

1. "Yes, please."

2. "Hello."

3. "No, thank you."

4. "Could you help me?"

5. "How are you?"

6. "May I have some space please?"

Here are some things that can be said to kids:

1. "Come here."

2. "Leave me alone."

3. "I don't want to talk right now."

4. "Cool!"

5. "Hey!"

6. "Wow!"

7. "Hi!"

Figure 5.1   Power Card

From *The Power Card Strategy: Using Special Interests to Motivate Children and Youth With Asperger Syndrome and Autism* by E. Gagnon (2001). Reprinted with permission from Autism Asperger Publishing Company, Shawnee Mission, KS.

The Power Card Strategy

The Power Card strategy in Figure 5.1 is a visual aid that uses a child's special interest to help her understand social situations, routines, the meaning of language, and the hidden curriculum (Gagnon, 2001). This intervention contains two components: a script and the Power Card. Using this approach, a teacher develops a brief script written at the child's comprehension level detailing the problem situation or target behavior. The script includes a description of the behavior and how the child's special interest addresses that social challenge. This solution is then generalized back to the child. The Power Card, the size of a business card or trading card, contains a picture of the special interest and a summary of the solution and is portable, to promote generalization. The Power Card can be carried, or it can be velcroed inside a book, notebook, or locker. It may also be placed on the corner of a child's desk (Gagnon, 2001).

This strategy has been empirically investigated with two children. In one case, the Power Card strategy resulted in marked behavior change and generalization across settings; a second child experienced moderate success when the Power Card strategy was used (Myles, Keeling, & Van Horn, 2001). Above is a Power Card used to help Jennifer, an 8-year-old girl, to remember to wash her hands. Jennifer's special interest was Angelica from the Rugrats. On the next page is a sample script.

Angelica Says, "Wash Those Hands"
  by Rachele M. Hill

Angelica knows how important it is to keep her hands clean. She does not want to catch any yucky germs from "those babies!" Germs can cause coughing, sneezing, and runny noses. Angelica definitely does not want to catch a cold! She washes her hands often and always after using the bathroom. She knows that washing her hands helps keep her from catching a cold.

Angelica wants you to have clean hands, too. She wants you to remember to wash your hands often and every time after you go to the bathroom.

Angelica wants you to remember these three things:

1. Wash your hands after you go to the bathroom.

2. Always use soap.

3. Dry your hands completely.

Angelica can be very bossy, but she does have manners when it comes to having clean hands. Angelica says, "Please wash your hands!"

Acting Lessons

Many adults with AS recommend acting lessons to teach social skills. During these lessons, children learn to express—verbally and nonverbally—emotions in specific situations. They also learn to interpret others' emotions, feelings, and voices. Perhaps most important, actors engage in simulations and receive feedback about their performance in an environment that positively supports practice. Acting lessons can be provided as a part of the school experience or in the community.

Self-Esteem Building

The child or youth with AS may look different, act different, feel different, and, in some ways, *is* different from other people. The child often knows this, and loss of self-esteem is often the by-product. As adults, there is a high price to pay for negative self-esteem, making it especially important to intervene and provide supports at an early age. For example, it has been documented that adults with AS have higher levels of depression, suicide, and other affective disorders than the general population, which can partially be related to self-concept problems (Williams, 2001; Wing, 1981).

Educators and parents must work together to help the child understand that she is more than the exceptionality. She is not AS! She is a child who has this exceptionality—but this is only one part of her. She has many other characteristics that must be pointed out and celebrated (Bieber, 1994). In fact, aspects other than the disorder should be the primary focus of a conversation about AS. The child with this exceptionality should understand that all people are special. Everyone does certain things well and finds others challenging. It is possible for the exceptionality to receive so much attention and focus that it becomes the major facet of the child's identity.

The child needs assistance to develop a positive self-image. This is built, in part, by successful experiences. LaVoie (cited in Bieber, 1994) poignantly challenges teachers and parents to find the "island of competence" in the child, stress it, and celebrate it. Presenting multiple opportunities for the child to demonstrate his "island of competence" builds self-esteem.

Strategies for building self-esteem include:

1. Place the child with AS in the role of helper or tutor to another student.
2. Tell the child what he is doing right. Reframe negative language to positive language.
3. Find out what the child does well and help her do more of it.
4. Compliment the child and teach him to compliment himself.

Ledgin (2002) has a different idea about helping individuals with AS develop positive self-esteem. In his book *Asperger's and Self-Esteem: Insight and Hope Through Famous Role Models,* he has identified 13 adults who seem to share some of the characteristics of AS. Among these role models are Charles Darwin, Carl Sagan, Albert Einstein, and Marie Curie. Ledgin's message is that although individuals with AS have challenges, there is hope for their future.

Self-Awareness

Self-awareness includes the ability to read and self-monitor positive and negative reactions. Children and youth with AS often have difficulty interpreting their emotions and social well-being. In fact, research has shown that adolescents with AS are not reliable reporters of personal stress, anxiety, or depression. This is not because they are avoiding an uncomfortable situation or misleading themselves or others, but rather because they often cannot tell when they are feeling these emotions (Barnhill, Hagiwara, Myles, Simpson, et al., 2000). Therefore, it is important to provide them with strategies that will help them understand their emotions and react in an appropriate manner to them. Two instructional strategies address this very important topic. The first, by McAfee (2002), works well with older students and educators who have substantial time to help students develop these skills. The second, by Buron and Curtis (2003), is a streamlined version developed for younger children for use in the home and school.

McAfee (2002) has developed a visually based curriculum designed to assist students to decrease stress by recognizing emotions and redirecting themselves to a calming activity. Through the use of a Stress Tracking Chart, a Summary of Stress Signals Worksheet, and a Stress Thermometer, students with AS learn how to

- Identify and label their emotions using nonverbal and situational cues
- Assign appropriate values to different degrees of emotion, such as anger
- Redirect negative thoughts to positive thoughts
- Identify environmental stressors and common reactions to them
- Recognize the early signs of stress
- Select relaxation techniques that match their needs

For examples of worksheets designed by McAfee (2002) for a student she refers to as Scott W, see Figures 5.2, 5.3, and 5.4.

Buron and Curtis (2003) created the Incredible 5-Point Scale to help individuals with AS understand themselves. The scale is unique in that it can be used as an obsessional index, a stress scale, a meltdown monitor, and so on. Children and youth with AS are taught to recognize the stages of their specific behavioral challenges and learn methods to self-calm at each level. Figure 5.5 provides an illustration of how the Incredible 5-Point Scale may be used.

Similarly, Faherty (2000) created a workbook for children and youth with AS to help them learn about themselves. Specifically, it facilitates self-awareness through a series of exercises, such as the one presented below:

Feeling Anxious

Everyone feels anxious sometimes. Anxious means that a person feels worried and confused. He might cry or his hands might tremble, or he might get a stomach ache or a headache. Sometimes he feels like running away or hiding. Sometimes feeling anxious makes people feel angry and they might want to scream and yell. Others might get very, very quiet when they are anxious.

Figure 5.2 Stress Tracking Chart

Stress Tracking Chart

Home/School

Student: Scott W.

Date & Time	Precipitating Event (trigger)	Underlying or "Hidden" Stressor(s) and Related Emotions	Stress Signals			Outcome
			Body Language, Facial Expressions & Verbal Cues (as observed)	Physical Symptoms (by student report)	Stress Level: Low, Moderate, High	
4/1/00 9:30 am	Ian sat in Scott's usual chair during art class	Anxiety due to schedule changes that week	Playing with hair Humming	Not obtainable	Moderate	Shoved Ian • Sent to principal
4/2/00 10:10 am	Joe borrowed Scott's pencil and then lost it	Angry because he was teased on the school bus that morning	Jaws and teeth clenched Squinting	Muscles tense Increased heart rate	High	Shouted swear word Threw paperwork on floor • Sent to principal
4/5/00 2:30 pm	Scott didn't finish math problems before class ended	Frustrated, unable to concentrate due to noise from photocopy machine in next room	Humming Tapping on desk Playing with hair	Headache Stomach ache	Moderate	Shouted at teacher that he "had to finish" • Points taken off math grade
4/6/00 1:30 pm	Bill accidentally bumped into Scott on playground at lunch	On playground for entire lunchtime. Difficulty joining in with other kids. Frustrated, lonely	Humming Glaring	Not obtainable	Moderate	Yelled at Bill and complained to playground aid • No further consequences
4/7/00 10:05 am	Teacher gently corrected Scott's verbal answer in class	Some other students had giggled last period when Scott was reading report in front of class	Teeth & fists clenched Squinting Talking loud and fast	Face hot Muscles tense Stomach ache	High	Fumed out of room yelling. "I don't like any of you" • Discussion with teacher
4/8/00 3:15 pm	Joe slapped Scott on the back as a nice 'hello' in hall	Group art project in afternoon	Hunched over	Headache Muscles tense Stomach ache	Low	Scowled at other student • No further consequences
4/9/00 12:30 pm	Working on grammar assignment	Photocopy machine in next room	Glazed expression Quiet	Shoulder muscles tense Mild headache	Low	Unable to focus on work

89

Figure 5.3   Summary of Stress Signals

Summary of Stress Signals

Student: _Scott W._

	Low Stress	Moderate Stress	High Stress
Verbal & nonverbal clues Body language, facial expressions & verbal clues (As observed by others. Data from Stress Tracking Charts)	Hunched-over posture Quiet, high-pitched voice Glazed expression	Humming Playing with hair Glares Tapping fingers on desk	Teeth clenched Fists clenched Squinting Talks loud & fast Pacing
Physical symptoms (As reported by student. Data from Stress Tracking Charts)	Shoulder muscles tense Mild headache	Muscles tense generally Stomach ache Headache	Muscles very tense Stomach ache Sweaty palms Breathing very fast Increased heart rate Face hot

From *Navigating the Social Work: A Curriculum for Individuals with Asperger's Syndrome, High Functioning Autism and Related Disorders,* by J. McAfee, 2002. Copyright 2002 by Future Horizons, Arlington, TX. Reprinted with permission.

Children with autism seem to get anxious more often than other people. I will mark what is true for me.

I feel anxious when:

- There is too much happening at the same time.
- Something is just not the way it's supposed to be.
- I don't want to do something different.
- There is too much noise or bright light.
- I feel sick.
- I don't understand something.
- Someone is talking too much.
- There are too many people around; I need to be alone.
- I don't know what to do.
- I can't find the words to say.
- I make a mistake.

Figure 5.4   Stress Thermometer

Stress Signals:		10		Relaxation Techniques:
		9		*High Stress*
teeth & fists clenched				
squints				swing
talks loud & fast		8		"walk, no talk"
paces				break time–go to quiet place
		7		
		6		*Moderate Stress*
hums		5		
plays with hair				listen to relaxing music
glares at other people				use Thera-putty
taps fingers on desk		4		break time–go to quiet place
		3		*Low Stress*
		2		
hunched-over posture				
quieter than usual				visualize being at beach
glazed expression		1		close eyes, put head down on desk
high-pitched voice				roll shoulders & neck

For: Scott W.

From *What Does It Mean to Me? A Workbook Explaining Self-Awareness and Life Lessons to the Child or Youth With High Functioning Autism or Asperger's Syndrome,* by J. C. Flaherty, 2002. Copyright 2002 by Future Horizons, Arlington, TX. Reprinted with permission.

- I want to be alone.
- Other:

The book *What Is Asperger Syndrome, and How Will It Affect Me? A Guide for Young People* (Ives, 2001) also helps young people to understand their AS. While acknowledging that it is often difficult to explain AS to others and that people will generally not be able to tell if somebody has AS just by looking at them, the book sends a positive yet realistic message to adolescents. Ives (2001) concluded the book with these statements to young people with AS:

It is important to remember that you are not alone. There are many people with Asperger syndrome. People with Asperger syndrome can go on to achieve a lot of things, including going to a university, getting a good job, living in their own house. You will always have Asperger syndrome although, as time goes on, you may get better at

Figure 5.5   Sample Incredible 5–Point Scale

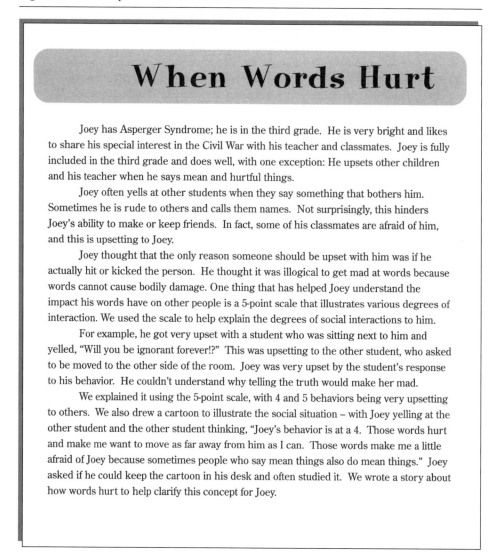

When Words Hurt

Joey has Asperger Syndrome; he is in the third grade. He is very bright and likes to share his special interest in the Civil War with his teacher and classmates. Joey is fully included in the third grade and does well, with one exception: He upsets other children and his teacher when he says mean and hurtful things.

Joey often yells at other students when they say something that bothers him. Sometimes he is rude to others and calls them names. Not surprisingly, this hinders Joey's ability to make or keep friends. In fact, some of his classmates are afraid of him, and this is upsetting to Joey.

Joey thought that the only reason someone should be upset with him was if he actually hit or kicked the person. He thought it was illogical to get mad at words because words cannot cause bodily damage. One thing that has helped Joey understand the impact his words have on other people is a 5-point scale that illustrates various degrees of interaction. We used the scale to help explain the degrees of social interactions to him.

For example, he got very upset with a student who was sitting next to him and yelled, "Will you be ignorant forever!?" This was upsetting to the other student, who asked to be moved to the other side of the room. Joey was very upset by the student's response to his behavior. He couldn't understand why telling the truth would make her mad.

We explained it using the 5-point scale, with 4 and 5 behaviors being very upsetting to others. We also drew a cartoon to illustrate the social situation – with Joey yelling at the other student and the other student thinking, "Joey's behavior is at a 4. Those words hurt and make me want to move as far away from him as I can. Those words make me a little afraid of Joey because sometimes people who say mean things also do mean things." Joey asked if he could keep the cartoon in his desk and often studied it. We wrote a story about how words hurt to help clarify this concept for Joey.

(Continued)

Figure 5.5   Sample Incredible 5–Point Scale

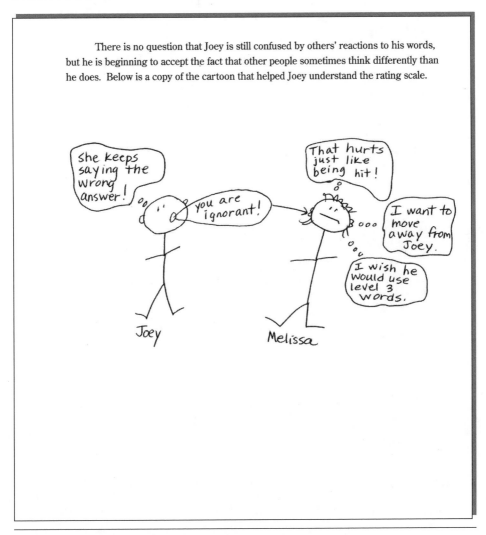

From *The Incredible Five-Point Scale: Assisting Students With Autism Spectrum Disorders in Understanding Social Interactions and Controlling Their Emotional Responses,* by K. Buron and M. Curtis (2003). Reprinted with permission from Autism Asperger Publishing Company, Shawnee Mission, KS.

Figure 5.6   Sample Incredible 5–Point Scale

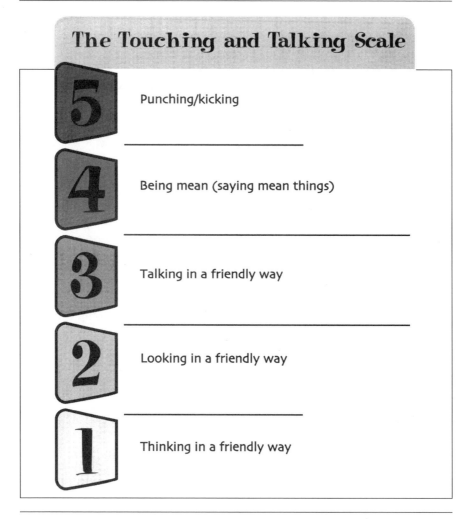

From *The Incredible Five-Point Scale: Assisting Students With Autism Spectrum Disorders in Understanding Social Interactions and Controlling Their Emotional Responses*, by K. Buron and M. Curtis (2003). Reprinted with permission from Autism Asperger Publishing Company, Shawnee Mission, KS.

things you used to find really hard. . . . Most importantly, remember that you are exactly the same person you always were, before you ever heard the words Asperger syndrome. Only now you have a way of understanding why you find some things tricky, and also can find ways of making life easier for yourself. (p. 20)

Finally, *This is Asperger Syndrome* (Gagnon & Myles, 1999) fosters self-understanding for younger children by presenting several scenarios from a day in the life of a child with Asperger Syndrome. It depicts how the child sees himself and others in social situations and discusses how others may have different perceptions, as illustrated in Figure 5.6.

Figure 5.7   Sample Scenario From *This Is Asperger Syndrome*

My teacher says I'm rude. I think I'm honest. I don't understand
why I can't tell someone that they have bad breath, ugly hair, or
to go away because I'm busy.
This is Asperger Syndrome.

From *This is Asperger Syndrome and Adolescence: Practical Solutions for School Success*, by B. S. Myles and
D. Andreon (2001). Reprinted with permission from Autism Asperger Publishing Company, Shawnee
Mission, KS.

Circle of Friends

Some children and adolescents with AS are fortunate enough to
belong to a small group of friends who look after each other. Having a
group of friends often makes the difference between success and failure for
youths with AS.

It is important to make sure that individuals with AS develop a social network, as this does not occur naturally. If the Circle of Friends concept is used,
it is recommended that more than one teen be involved. Individuals who
make up the Circle of Friends should be (a) high-status peers, (b) generally
compliant with school rules, (c) socially astute, and (d) genuinely
interested in (and, hopefully, like) the student with AS. Individuals who
enjoy the way persons with AS look at life are excellent candidates for a
Circle of Friends. Moreover, those who participate in the circle must value
the person with AS, not merely placate and direct her (Myles & Simpson,

2003). It is sometimes easier to recruit young girls than boys to be in a Circle of Friends, as they tend to be more nurturing and sensitive to the needs of others at this age. However, if high-status girls, such as cheerleaders, drill team members, or athletes, participate in a Circle of Friends, neurotypical boys will generally follow.

It is important to provide AS awareness training to ensure success in a Circle of Friends. While it is not important that the term "AS" be used, it is essential that the "friends" understand the individual with AS and how they can best become friends. Parents of the youth with AS should be involved in developing a Circle of Friends and awareness training. Some parents include the students with AS in the awareness training. Others have made the opposite decision, asking the peer group not to say that they are a Circle of Friends. Some parents have even paid students to participate in Circle of Friends activities after school. It is preferable, however, to facilitate relationships that have a chance to develop into true friendships without such external reinforcement.

Establishing a Lunch Bunch is one way of using a Circle of Friends. Lilia, a middle-school student with AS, participates in a Lunch Bunch and eats lunch each day with three or four students her age. The peers interact with her as a friend, helping her participate in lunch conversation, for example. The conversation is natural (about school, friends, television shows, etc.) and the friends make sure that Lilia asks and answers questions. They have also used the Lunch Bunch to make Lilia more aware of how other teens dress and what they like to talk about—a great way for adolescents with AS to learn more about the hidden curriculum.

Interpretation

Social situations occur daily or even hourly that make little or no sense to persons with AS but are taken for granted by the general population. These individuals often end up in trouble because they are unable to understand a direction or intent. Even when the person with AS receives effective instruction in the social and behavioral realms, situations will occur that require interpretation. Several interpretive strategies can help turn seemingly random actions into meaningful interactions for individuals with AS. These include (a) cartooning; (b) social autopsies; (c) the Situation, Options, Consequences, Choices, Strategies, Simulation (SOCCSS) strategy; and (d) sensory awareness. These strategies are important because they are designed to help students understand and self-monitor their behavior, social skills, and situations in which they participate.

Figure 5.8   Sample Cartoon

Cartooning

Cartooning is a generic terms that has been used for years by speech-language pathologists to describe the drawing they do to explain situations, events, or language terms (such as idioms or metaphors) to their clients. According to Arwood and Brown (1999), a cartoon is used to

- explain and change behavior
- improve social skills
- manage time
- improve academic skills
- help students clarify or refine their ideas

According to Gray (1995), cartoons, which she calls *comic strip conversations,* illustrate and interpret social situations and provide support to "students who struggle to comprehend the quick exchange of information which occurs in a conversation" (p. 1). They promote social understanding by incorporating simple figures and other symbols in a comic strip format. Speech, conversation bubble symbols, and color are used to help the individual with AS see and analyze a conversation. Figure 5.7 is a cartoon that was drawn after a young man with AS mistakenly thought the greeting "How Ya doin' dog" was an insult.

Social Autopsies

The social autopsy was developed by Lavoie (cited in Bieber, 1994) as a way to help students with social problems understand social mistakes. Simply stated, the social autopsy is a vehicle for analyzing a social skills problem. Following a social problem or mistake, the student who committed the error works with an adult to (a) identify the error, (b) determine who was harmed by the error, (c) decide how to correct the error, and (d) develop a plan so that the error does not occur again. A social skills autopsy is not a punishment. It is a supportive problem-solving strategy. It teaches cause and effect and allows a student to see how his behavior impacts others (Bieber, 1994). Every adult with whom the student with AS has regular contact, such as parents, bus drivers, teachers, custodians, and cafeteria workers, should know how to do a social skills autopsy to help foster skill acquisition and generalization. A blank social autopsies worksheet appears in Figure 5.9. A social autopsies worksheet completed by a teacher and a child with AS is shown in Figure 5.10. The worksheet outlines what happened when Arthur belched aloud in class and what he could do the next time he had to burp.

Situation-Options-Consequences-Choices-
Strategies-Simulation (SOCCSS)

Jan Roosa (personal communication, April 22, 1995) developed the Situation-Options-Consequences-Choices-Strategies-Simulation (SOCCSS) strategy to help students with social disabilities understand social situations and develop problem-solving skills by putting social and behavioral issues into a sequential form. This teacher-directed strategy helps students understand cause and effect and realize that they can influence the outcome of many situations by the decisions they make. The strategy can be used one on one with a student or can take place as a group activity, depending on the situation and students' needs. The six steps of SOCCSS are as follows:

1. SITUATION: After a social problem occurs, the teacher helps the student to identify who, what, when, where, and why. Who was involved in the situation? What actually happened? When did it happen? Where did the problem occur? Why did it happen? The goal is to encourage the student to relate these variables independently. However, at first the teacher assumes an active role in prompting and identifying, when necessary, the answers to these questions.

2. OPTIONS: The teacher and student brainstorm several behavioral options the student could have chosen. Brainstorming means that

(Text continues on page 101)

Figure 5.9   Social Autopsies Worksheet

Social Autopsies Worksheet

What happened? _____

_____

_____

_____

What was the social error?	Who was hurt by the social error?

What should be done to correct the error? _____

_____

_____

_____

What could be done next time? _____

_____

_____

_____

_____

_____

_____

Developed by: Eileen Gorup and Jeanne Holverstott

Figure 5.10   Completed Social Autopsies Worksheet

Social Autopsies Worksheet

What happened?   <u>I belched when called on to answer a question in class.</u>

What was the social error?	Who was hurt by the social error?
Belching in class	classmates
	teacher
	me

What should be done to correct the error? _____
   <u>If I need to belch I will cover my mouth and say excuse me.</u>

What could be done next time? _____
   <u>I will cover my mouth and say excuse me, then answer the question.</u>
   <u>If I know in advance that I am going to burp, I will cover my mouth</u>
   <u>and try to belch silently.</u>
   <u>Burping is not a funny joke, even if the other kids laugh.</u>
   <u>Many people think belching out loud is rude.</u>

Developed by: Eileen Gorup and Jeanne Holverstott

the teacher accepts and records all student responses without evaluating them. Initially, the teacher usually has to encourage the student to identify more than one thing he could have done or said differently.

3. CONSEQUENCES: For each behavior option generated, a consequence is listed. For example, the teacher asks the student, "So what would happen if you *(name the option)?"* Some options may have more than one consequence. It is often difficult for students with AS to generate consequences because of their difficulty determining cause-and-effect relationships. Role-play at this stage can serve as a prompt in identifying the consequence.

4. CHOICES: Options and consequences are prioritized using a numerical sequence or a yes/no response. Following prioritization, the student is prompted to select the option that she thinks (a) she will be able to do and (b) will most likely get her what she wants or needs.

5. STRATEGIES: The next step is to develop a plan to carry out the option if the *situation* occurs. Although the teacher and youth collaborate on the stages of the plan, the student should generate the plan. This is important because the student must feel that he has been the decision maker and is responsible for the plan.

6. SIMULATION: Practice is the sixth stage in SOCCSS. Roosa has defined this practice in a variety of ways: (a) using imagery, (b) talking with another about the plan, (c) writing down the plan, or (d) role-playing. Regardless of the method used, the student ends up evaluating his impressions of the simulation. Did the simulation activity give him the skills and confidence to carry out the plan? If the answer is "no," additional simulation must take place.

Although designed as interpretive—it is used after the fact—this strategy can also be used as an instructional strategy. That is, teachers can identify problems students are likely to encounter and address them using SOCCSS so that students have a plan prior to a situation occurring (Myles & Simpson, 2001, 2003; Myles & Southwick, 1999). A blank worksheet to facilitate the SOCCSS process appears in Figure 5.10. Figure 5.11 contains a completed SOCCSS worksheet that was used with Ted, who had gotten in trouble for cursing but did not understand why.

Sensory Awareness

All the information we receive from the environment comes through our sensory system. Thus the senses of taste, smell, sight, sound, touch, movement, gravity force, and balance impact learning (Ayres, 1979). As mentioned earlier, many individuals with AS have sensory problems and therefore require direct assistance in this area (Dunn et al., 2002). Several

Figure 5.11   SOCCSS Worksheet

Situation			
Who _____		When _____	
What _____		Why _____	
_____			

Options	Consequences	Choice

Strategy - Plan of Action

Simulation	Select One
1. Find a quiet place, sit back, and imagine how your Situation would work (or not work) based on the various Options and Consequences.	
2. Talk with a peer, staff, or other person about your plan of action.	
3. Write down on paper what may happen in your Situation based on your Options and Consequences.	
4. Practice your Options with one or more people using behavior rehearsal. Start simple and easy for learning. Only make it difficult to test the learning.	
5. _____ _____	

Simulation Outcomes

Follow-Up

Developed by: Eileen Gorup

From *This is Asperger Syndrome and Adolescence: Practical Solutions for School Success,* by B. S. Myles and D. Andreon (2001). Reprinted with permission from Autism Asperger Publishing Company, Shawnee Mission, KS.

Figure 5.12   Sample SOCCSS Worksheet

Situation

Who <u>Ted</u>   **Where** <u>Middle school hallway</u>   **When** <u>During 2nd and 3rd Hour passing period</u>

What <u>Ted was talking to a friend using curse words and the principal called him to the office.</u>

Why <u>Ted noticed others using words and thought it would impress his peers.</u>

Options	Consequences	Choice
I Can talk quietly so the principal cannot hear me.	The principal would not have heard me and I would not have gotten in trouble.	No
Ask a teacher or adult if the words the others are using are okay.	I would have found out the words were not okay to use.	Yes/2
Talk to my friends using nice words.	I would not have gotten into trouble.	Yes/1
Do not use curse words around adults.	I still could have been caught, if an adult heard me.	No

---

Strategy - Plan of Action

During my next passing period I will talk with my friends using appropriate words.

Simulation	Select One
1. Find a quiet place, sit back, and imagine how your Situation will work (or not work) based on the various Options and Consequences	
2. Talk with a peer, staff, or other person about your plan of action.	I will talk to my principal
3. Write down on paper what may happen in your Situation based on your Options and Consequences.	
4. Practice your Options with one or more people using behavior rehearsal. Start simple and easy for learning. Only make it difficult to test the learning.	
5. _____ _____	

Simulation Outcomes

Ted met with the principal and discussed his "plan of action". The principal and Ted agreed that this was a great plan and he would help monitor Ted in the hallways during passing period.

Follow-Up

Since this situation Ted has not used curse words at school.

Developed by: Eileen Gorup

From *This is Asperger Syndrome and Adolescence: Practical Solutions for School Success,* by B. S. Myles and D. Andreon (2001). Reprinted with permission from Autism Asperger Publishing Company, Shawnee Mission, KS.

programs, including those mentioned below, appear effective in meeting the sensory needs of children and youth with AS.

The Tool Chest for Teachers, Parents, and Students (Henry Occupational Therapy Services, 1998) emphasizes behavior as a means of communication and helps adult users to develop sensory strategies that prevent students' behavior problems. Two videotapes supplement the program by demonstrating important strategies.

Building Bridges Through Sensory Integration (Yack, Sutton, & Aquilla, 1998) discusses the role of occupational therapy and sensory integration specifically for persons with autism or other pervasive developmental disorders. User-friendly checklists identify sensory issues that are subsequently addressed through a series of activities provided in the curriculum.

Asperger Syndrome and Sensory Issues: Practical Solutions for Making Sense of the World (Myles, Cook, et al., 2000) is the only book that specifically addresses the sensory problems experienced by individuals with AS. The book overviews the impact of sensory challenges on the academic, social, and behavioral domains and introduces strategies that are easy to use in general education settings.

Coaching

The third step in social support is coaching—helping children and youth with AS actually use the skills they have developed during social skills instruction and interpretation. Because these individuals often cognitively know skills but cannot apply them, this step is essential. Upon observing the child in a social situation, a coach—educator, parent, mental health professional, or older child—can unobtrusively prompt the child to use specific skills. Coaching a child or adolescent with AS requires that the individual understand the delicate balance between (a) providing support via coaching when needed and (b) allowing the student to independently use skills that she has mastered. Coaching should only be provided after the coach is certain that the child needs support to use a social skill. Coaching can take several forms: (a) feeding the language, (b) conversation starters, and (c) video modeling.

Feeding the Language

Adults who feed the language (Collins, personal communication, February 5, 1999) to children with AS are verbally prompting them toward a social activity. The prompt may be an inconspicuous verbatim statement that the child is to say. That is, the adult is extremely discreet when he feeds the language. Only the child with AS knows that he is being

Assistive Technology Supports

6

by Sean J. Smith, Mariangeles Murphy-Herd,
Daniel Alvarado, and Nancy Glennon

CASE STUDY: NOLAN

Nolan, a fifth-grade student with AS, has a reading disability. When given verbal instructions or oral exams, Nolan performs at a higher level than most of his classmates if he recites or types his answers. Nolan often receives grades in the D/D+ range when he has to respond to test items using a paper and pencil format.

CASE STUDY: TONY

Tony, a seventh-grade student, likes to socialize with his peers. Every morning before the first bell rings for homeroom, Tony talks to classmates about the latest episode of Yu-Gi-Oh. The others are also interested in Yu-Gi-Oh, but Tony dominates the conversation and his peers think that Tony is bragging. When his peers attempt to change the topic of conversation away from Yu-Gi-Oh, Tony persists in talking about this topic. As a result, Tony's classmates don't want to include him in their conversations. Tony does not understand why his peers do not want to talk to him.

In attempting to meet the diverse needs of students with AS, parents, teachers, and related professionals are challenged with identifying and integrating the right "tools" to ensure classroom success. Over the past two decades, technology applications have increasingly become a part of the instructional solution. For all students with disabilities served under the *Individuals with Disabilities Education Act* (IDEA), technology, or better yet, assistive technology, is a critical ingredient in the overall growth and development process.

The growth in technology opens up wonderful opportunities for educators and *all* students. But there is one major distinction. For students without disabilities, technology often makes things *easier;* for students with disabilities, technology makes things *possible* (e.g., access to the general education classroom). This chapter will offer an overview of assistive technology, what is required, a framework for identifying and selecting appropriate assistive technology tools, and a sampling of software, hardware, and Internet-based solutions that have been found to assist individuals with AS.

ASSISTIVE TECHNOLOGY DEFINITION

"Assistive technology device" was defined first in the *Technology-Related Assistance for Individuals with Disabilities Act* of 1988 (P.L. 100–407), better known as the "Tech Act," and the definition was included later in the 1990 reauthorization of the *Individuals with Disabilities Education Act* (IDEA). In 1990, Congress identified assistive technology (AT) as a critical instrument in meeting the educational and overall developmental needs of students with disabilities in school. This definition of AT is broad, allowing for variability in the types of devices and technology applications that can be used. For example, an electronic wheelchair for a child with mobility limitations as well as a PDA for a child with organizational problems are equally supported and covered under this legislation.

Many special educators have argued that there are three components of the definition of an AT device: what it is, how it is made, and its use.

- "What" refers to the device and what it actually is (e.g., an alternative communication device, word processing application, a text-to-speech application).
- "How" refers to how one acquires the device. Was it purchased at the local computer store, was an existing device modified, or was it customized to meet the specific needs (e.g., language, social skill development) of the individual?
- "Use" refers to the actual purpose of the device specifically for the user. For a device to be applicable, it must sustain a functioning level or enhance the person's current functioning. For example, a PDA may help a student get better grades because she can record her homework on the device and subsequently complete it.

What type of devices apply or are included under the umbrella of assistive technology? The simple answer is almost any device that enhances or maintains the functional needs of the individual with a disability. AT devices can be grouped into seven categories: positioning, mobility, augmentative and alternative communication, computer access, adaptive toys and games, adaptive environments, and instructional aids (Bryant & Bryant, 2004).

For our purposes, technology for most students with AS falls under the last category: instructional aids to support communication, social interaction, and organization. Instructional aids include technology that is used to compensate for limited organizational skills (e.g., AlphaSmart, PDA) or technology that is used for remediation purposes (e.g., language or reading instructional programs). Whatever the application, the broad category, and one that continually expands as technology grows, involves devices and adaptations that help facilitate learning in one way or another.

Assistive Technology Services

The Tech Act of IDEA legislation also includes language specific to assistive technology services. AT service is a term that has been defined as any service that directly assists an individual with a disability in the selection, acquisition, or use of an assistive technology device:

- Functional evaluation of the person in the individual's customary environment
- Purchasing or leasing
- Selecting, designing, fitting
- Coordinating and using other therapies or interventions
- Training or technical assistance for an individual with disabilities or the family
- Training or technical assistance for a professional

AT services are critical to the identification, implementation, and evaluation of the AT device. That is, without services, students, teachers, parents, and related service personnel would not be able to effectively identify appropriate technology applications, integrate them into the lives of students, and measure their effectiveness in maintaining or enhancing a student's functional abilities. Similarly, AT services assist teachers and parents in acquiring a device and receiving appropriate training and support to ensure the device is right for the student and can be used in the appropriate environments. In the following discussion, we will attempt to bring meaning to the various elements of AT services and how they apply to the classroom and community-based setting, with particular reference to students with AS.

Instructional Technology

Instructional technology refers to any technology that is used in the education of an individual. Thus the term includes everything from presentation software and hardware used by teachers and students to multimedia software and the Internet. Software and hardware that can assist students and teachers to remediate academic or content weaknesses are also included. Consequently, many, if not all, instructional technologies can be considered assistive technologies. In the case study, Nolan has a reading disability. To assist him to improve his reading he uses a reading instructional software program (e.g., Read 180). Nolan uses the instructional software and hardware (a computer and tape recorder) to increase his functioning (reading) capabilities. While some students may find the same software and hardware to be *helpful,* for Nolan it is *assistive,* that is, an AT device.

Comparing assistive technology to instructional technology may appear peculiar. That is, when thinking of AT devices, many picture mobility aids, devices to augment speech, or Braille readers to help those who are blind. It is important to realize that many of these "traditional" assistive technology devices meet the needs of a limited number of children with identified disabilities. For the majority of children being served under IDEA, AT is focused on learning (e.g., learning disabilities), social and emotional (e.g., AS), and language considerations (e.g., communication disorders). Thus recent legislative and instructional changes have sought to further the use of technology with individuals with "mild" disabilities (e.g., AS, learning disabilities, attention challenges).

In 1997, the reauthorization of the IDEA reinforced the need to consider AT devices for all children with disabilities by requiring each IEP team to consider whether AT devices were necessary for the specific student with a disability. Thus on every IEP one will find a place where the team is asked to note that AT was considered for the child and his or her educational needs. This is critical in that it forces educators and parents to truly examine software and hardware applications that could improve learning, attention, organization, language, and behavior. Similarly, the AT service provision requires educators and parents to develop a plan that will mean successful identification, implementation, and evaluation of the device into the child's learning environment. Some would argue that the inclusion of the AT consideration requirement is an example of how technology is seen as a critical tool in the successful inclusion of all students in the general education setting.

FRAMEWORK FOR ASSISTIVE TECHNOLOGY SELECTION

As mentioned above, technology is a viable tool to provide access for individuals with disabilities. For students with AS, this means access to the general education classroom and the related academic, social, and behavioral requirements. Recognition of the instructional capabilities of AT has prompted an array of adaptations and solutions (e.g., word prediction software, handheld organizers, digitized books) to help students who have academic, social, and behavioral goals on their IEPs and to facilitate success in the general education setting and related extracurricular experiences.

Ultimately, the identification and implementation of the AT device depends on the knowledge and abilities of the IEP team. If team members are limited in their knowledge of AT devices, it is presumed that the use of AT in the life of the child will also be limited. To address this concern, educators must become aware of assessments and related frameworks that can assist them in identifying and selecting AT.

SETT Framework

One process that is increasingly being used by IEP teams is the SETT Framework. SETT is an acronym for Student, Environments, Tasks, and Tools. Basically, SETT offers IEP team members a structure so they can work together to better identify and select assistive technology devices and services that would meet the specific needs of a student, thus furthering access to educational opportunities.

The SETT framework is designed to be a collaborative experience where each person (e.g., parent, teacher, related service provider) shares his or her individual knowledge and expertise in order to build the team's collective knowledge of the student, the environments in which she functions, and the tasks the student has to be able to do (e.g., organizational, communication, learning) to be an active learner in those environments. The SETT framework provides a method for the team to acquire this knowledge, analyze specific needs, and consider what system of assistive technology tools (devices and services) is necessary for the student, in the identified environments, to do the expected tasks.

Why the need for the SETT framework? When assistive technology first emerged, it was widely believed that the right tool could be identified to meet the broad needs of the individual. However, it quickly became apparent that many of these tools were being underutilized or abandoned because they didn't meet the specific and unique needs of the individual and his environment. Meanwhile, the tremendous growth in AT devices has limited any one professional's ability to keep track of and fully understand what device or service is appropriate for a specific individual. As a result, many students with disabilities were not benefiting much from the early promise of assistive technology.

The key to the SETT framework is that each group member is seen as equal and as bringing critical expert knowledge to some area of the assistive technology solution. When using this framework, each person shares his or her individual knowledge of the student, the environments, and tasks in order to build the team's collective knowledge. Through this group interaction, teams can then use their collective knowledge to consider whether or not assistive technology tools are required by the student, and if they are, can develop a system of tools that are student-centered, environmentally useful, and specific to the student's need. For example, a student with difficulty organizing assignments, study materials, and the like would have multiple technology tools available to him or her for support (e.g., laptop computer, PDA). Through the SETT framework, a team would not only be able to identify the device that would best address the organizational challenges, but also classroom needs (e.g., small desk), school needs (e.g., transitions from class to class), and related concerns. By working through the SETT framework together, IEP team members develop a solid basis for tool selection, and at the same time, a shared vision of when and how the tools are supposed to be used by the student. A shared vision and parity among group members is critical for appropriate identification of the tool and, more importantly, for successful implementation and use of the tool by the student.

Assessment Instruments

While the SETT framework is critical to the identification and ultimate selection of the AT device, a thorough evaluation and assessment of assistive technology is sometimes needed. An effective assessment matches a person with a disability to the best available AT and usually requires more than one evaluation. Each evaluation looks at specific aspects based on the individual's needs, which may include augmentative communication, organizational skill development, mobility, environmental control, recreation, or computer access. No one person can do an assessment for all needs, so a team of specialists is usually required. All team members work closely with one another, and each team member makes a unique contribution. Not all specialists need to be available for a particular assessment.

Team members may include the individual with a disability and, where appropriate, family members or caregivers. They are the most important members of the team because they identify needs for technology and have a unique insight into what will work. While this assessment is often connected to the SETT framework, the actual assessment is conducted to identify strengths and weaknesses, determine progress, and provide data in order to select the appropriate device.

Individuals—other than the person with the disability and parents—often involved in a thorough AT assessment include:

- The occupational therapist (OT). Evaluates hand (fine motor) and total body (gross motor) skills, touch and movement abilities, visual perception, and positioning, and helps to find the person's best method to use AT.
- The physical therapist (PT). Evaluates seating, positioning, and mobility. The PT works closely with the OT and speech-language pathologist (SLP) to find the best position for the person to be in when using the technology.
- The speech-language pathologist. Evaluates the person's communication abilities. The SLP is very important in deciding the type of augmentative communication that will work.

A thorough assessment considers four major components:

- Tasks. The specific tasks or functions to be performed (e.g., reading, writing, remembering) and the requisite skills associated with the tasks.
- Context. The specific contexts of interaction (across settings such as school, home, work, and over time such as over a quarter, school year, or lifetime).
- Individual. The individual's strengths, weaknesses, abilities, prior experience, knowledge, and interests.
- Device. The specific device (e.g., reliability, operational ease, technical support, cost).

One of the more popular assessments is the Functional Evaluation for Assistive Technology (FEAT). This test offers a matching inventory, an individual scale, and a checklist of strengths and limitations as they apply to specific content and overall learning skills. Various state education agencies have developed their own assessment forms. For example, the Wisconsin Assistive Technology Initiative (WATI) (see http://www.wati .org/assesmentforms.htm) has received significant use by school districts across the country. Similarly, the Georgia Project for Assistive Technology (http://www.gpat.org/) offers a series of assessment protocols specific to content areas (e.g., reading, writing) as well as physical (e.g., vision, mobility) or communicative (e.g., augmentative communication) needs.

Figure 6.1   Assistive Technology Wheel

The Assistive Technology Consideration Quick Wheel was developed by the IDEA Local Implementation by Local Administrators (ILIAD) Partnership, the Technology and Media (TAM) Division of the Council for Exceptional Children, and the Wisconsin Assistive Technology Initiative. To purchase, contact the Council for Exceptional Children (1-888-232-7733; http://www.cec.sped.org). Permission to reprint photographs of the AT Quick Wheel obtained from the Council for Exceptional Children.

Various organizations and professional groups have also developed versions of assessment protocols and checklists to assist professionals and parents in identifying and selecting assistive technology devices and services. For instance, the Council for Exceptional Children's Technology and Media Division recently developed the AT Wheel (see Figure 6.1), which offers quick and easy access to AT information specific to a learning need. Regardless of the assessment form used, it is critical that an instrument be considered to structure the identification and selection process.

Providing professionals and parents quick access to technology solutions for students with disabilities, the Assistive Technology Consideration Quick Wheel is an easy-to-use tool for all. Developed in collaboration with the Wisconsin Assistive Technology Initiative, the U.S. Department of Education's Office of Special Education Programs, and the Council for Exceptional Children's Technology and Media Division, the AT Wheel collapses information found on a variety of checklists and skill protocol assessment forms specific to assistive technology. Instead of a lengthy form, the AT Wheel allows professionals and parents to identify an area of need (e.g., learning and studying, composing written material). For example, for a child with AS who has difficulty with learning, the AT Wheel lists twelve possible solutions to choose from. Ordered in a low technology (low tech) to high technology (high tech) continuum, users can review the list and consider possible tools appropriate for the needs of the child. One low-tech solution involves "highlighting text" as the learner reviews relevant material. For those that require additional support, an "electronic organizer" might be more appropriate. For someone with more significant needs, a handheld computer is offered as the high-tech solution. Of course, these suggestions are only some of the many tools available; however, the list helps the user get started. Similarly, the list offers potential tools but does not negate the need for further examination and student trial. Finally, the center of the AT Wheel offers a complete definition of what is considered an assistive technology device and service. On the opposite side of the AT Wheel is a list of books, journals, newsletters, and Internet sites applicable to assistive technology.

ASSISTIVE TECHNOLOGY SOLUTIONS

Once an IEP team has identified strengths as well as areas that present challenges, it is important to devise a plan that includes all of the tools teachers and parents wish to try. There is never enough time to try every tool. However, by carefully looking at a student's needs and strengths, it is possible to create a plan with a carefully chosen variety of low-, mid-, and high-tech tools. Edyburn (2000) and Sweeney (2003) would argue this is similar to the way a builder examines her toolbox. That is, if the builder's toolbox simply contained a hammer, she would be in trouble. Similarly, students with disabilities, particularly those with AS, require a variety of tools for different tasks and needs depending on content, environment, grade level and the like. In the past, it was often thought that it was enough to identify one good technology tool for the student. However, providing a student with just one tool means that he will probably end up doing no better than "painting with a hammer!" Instead, to meet the student's needs, professionals must consider a continuum of AT tools and devices.

The AT continuum can simply be a one-page summary to use during an IEP planning session to assist members as they focus on areas of challenge defined by the task, the need associated with that task, and the different environments in which that task is done. Upon understanding these components, as discussed above, the IEP team should decide on an AT solution based on a full continuum of low- to high-tech tools.

Sweeney (2003) defines a low-tech tool as:

- Less restrictive
- "Looks" closer to what everyone else is doing and using
- Easier to train with and use

Low-tech tools are often less expensive than other technology solutions and do not require an investment of time and prior knowledge to be used immediately. For example, a student with AS who has difficulty organizing class work and related assignments may need to use color-coded notebooks, folders, and paper to better structure her learning. Highlighters, colored pens and pencils, and similar writing aides might also be helpful. A tape recorder might be useful for students to record lectures to listen to later. There are ergonomic pens and pencils available for students to assist with fine- or gross-motor concerns (see http://www.ergonomicsconsulting.com). Low-tech solutions may also include altered room lighting (e.g., natural light) and other less intrusive tools. It is critical to start out with low-tech solutions as primary considerations. Often they can be immediately applied and are flexible to modify and easy to use without altering class instruction.

Mid-tech tools include handheld devices and many tools that require batteries. For example, handheld calculators, spell checkers, and reading dictionaries (e.g., Homework Wiz) are becoming increasingly popular for all students, especially those with disabilities (see http://www.franklin.com). For the student who needs assistance with taking notes, composing thoughts, and writing papers, handheld tape recorders are frequently used. Note taking and organizing can be further enhanced through portable word processors (e.g., AlphaSmart) as well as portable handheld scanners. Regardless of the mid-tech tool used, a major advantage is that these devices are becoming more and more available and are being used by students, their parents, and siblings. Thus such devices are generally accessible and often tools that are used willingly by students with AS.

On the far end of the technology continuum lie high-tech tools that offer great assistance but often

- Are restrictive to specific needs
- Are unique and different from typical technology used in the classroom
- Require extensive training to use and maintain

High-tech tools are often specialized to the specific needs of the student and thus generally cost more and require additional support. For example, a student with significant communication concerns may require an augmentative communication device like one produced by Dynavox Systems (see http://www.dynavoxsys.com). These tools help people with speech, language, learning, and physical disabilities communicate. Most require specific training to use and are programmed to the specific needs of the student. While they offer tremendous support and often make the difference between being able to access the general curriculum or not, the investment is quite substantial. Thus IEP teams must ensure through effective assessment that this technology is the appropriate solution for a given student.

TECHNOLOGY SOLUTIONS

Social Interaction Solutions

As mentioned in earlier chapters, individuals with AS have difficulty in the areas of social interaction, emotional reciprocity, developing peer relationships appropriate to their age, and sharing appropriately their social moments of enjoyment, interests, and achievements. These are skills that can be improved with direct instruction and through the application of technology. For example, word processing programs (e.g., Microsoft Word) can assist students in scripting potential conversations. That is, with assistance from a teacher, a SLP, or a parent, a student could preplan the appropriate things to say in a given situation. Students would be able to carry the script with them to practice in preparation for a particular situation. Further, as they prepare for and engage in the situation, they may check their script to modify their conversation. While extra effort and practice is involved, the script—or simply having access to the script—may allow the student to relax and concentrate on what has been taught and generalize the related social skills to a particular experience.

Social scripts are not the solution for all students. Instead, some students use social narratives as a possible solution. Social narratives can provide both guidance and direction for students in responding to various social situations. For some students, the text-based story may not offer enough context to generalize to a particular social situation. Instead, the use of pictures or illustrations may be critical in describing the situation (e.g., how one should feel or react, or what prompts the feelings or reactions). With technology, social narratives can come alive and offer the needed anchor. For example, simply taking and using digital pictures to illustrate the social situation may improve comprehension. The digital picture can be resized, reshaped, colored, and modified (e.g., Adobe Photoshop) as necessary to offer further application (see http://www.adobe.com).

To offer a more visual anchor, multimedia programs like HyperStudio (see http://www.hyperstudio.com), IntelliTools (see http://www.intell itools.com), and PowerPoint (see http://www.microsoft.com) may be used Using these tools, the narrative can "come alive" for the learner and improve her ability to generalize the story to an actual context or event. The Cognition and Technology Group at Vanderbilt (1993) refer to this as anchored instruction, or teaching that is situated in engaging, problem-rich environments that sustain exploration by students and teachers. The focus is on preventing inert knowledge by situated learning in the context of what one might refer to as authentic experiences and practical apprenticeships—activities that learners consider important. By offering a visual context for the learner through a multimedia application (e.g., HyperStudio), one provides the learner with a visual cue from which to build understanding.

In developing an interactive social narrative, students, teachers, paraprofessionals, and others can use the narrative multiple times, as necessary. Multimedia applications offer ongoing flexibility to modify and build upon the story with pictures (e.g., photographs, graphs), audio recording (e.g., the student's voice, peers, parents, teachers), video clips (e.g., the student completing components of the social activity), and similar interactive features.

For the student who requires specific social cues and ongoing development of social skills for specific situations, programs that offer organization and scripting of information are becoming increasingly widespread. Two incredibly popular applications among general and special education teachers across grade levels, and thus accessible to a variety of students, are *Inspiration* and *Kidspiration. Inspiration* (see http://www.inspiration .com), or *Kidspiration* (see http://www.kidspiration.com) for primary and early elementary grades, offers a visual structure to apply across situations. It allows the individual to break down topics into subtopics, however complex. For example, to better understand simple greetings, *Inspiration* can break down the process for the learner:

    I. Greetings
        1. First time you see a familiar person that day
            a. Good morning (if before noon)
            b. Good afternoon (after lunch)

      c. Hi

      d. How are you? (Wait for an answer 5 seconds, then go on)

  2. When you see an adult

      a. Good morning Mr. (Ms.) . . .

      b. Good afternoon Ms. (Mr.) . . .

      c. Hello

  3. When you see a friend your age

      a. Hi

      b. What's up?

      c. What's happening?

II. Conversation

  1. Starters: (Words you use to begin a conversation)

      a. What did you do last night?

      b. What's happening?

      c. Let me tell you what happened to me (to Mom, to Dad)

      d. Guess what?

  2. Continuers (words or sounds you use to let people know you are listening)

      a. Really!

      b. Good

      c. Yes

      d. That's great

      e. Uh huh

      f. I'm sorry

      g. That's too bad

      h. What did you do then?

  3. Words you use when you're finishing a conversation or leaving

      a. See you later

      b. Take care

      c. Gotta go now

For students with AS, *Inspiration* offers the ability to expand and contract the levels of the outline. Thus when an individual is working on learning appropriate responses, he can collapse a level and hide unnecessary information. Meanwhile, he can examine the appropriate category and identify the prompt that will recall examples of phrases he can use. In addition, since it is a digital outline, new phrases can easily be added, and outmoded ones taken away. For the visual learner, graphics can be used to illustrate positive or negative statements. For a younger child who is not a proficient reader, *Kidspiration* offers text-to-speech output for an auditory response. A similar organizer with audio output is *DraftBuilder* (see http://www.donjohnston.com). This software is similar to *Inspiration/ Kidspiration* in that it offers text-to-speech and organizational levels but does not provide users the ability to expand and contract an outline.

Because individuals with AS have trouble reading the emotions of others, body language, and facial expressions, it is helpful to have a way for them to look at photographs to determine how the person in the photograph is feeling. One program specifically designed for this is *Mindreading* (see http://www.human-emotions.com). Others have used the mind reading structure suggested in *Teaching Children with Autism to Mind Read* (Howlin, Baron-Coehn, & Hadwin, 1999) to create PowerPoint (see http://www.microsoft.com) activities that address teaching preschool children to recognize facial expression, emotions from line drawings, and to identify situation-based and desire-based emotions (Furick, 2003).

Finally, as mentioned in Chapter 5, teachers often use video of specific social situations that can be recorded earlier and then reviewed by the student and a related support person. In the case study, Tony has trouble with peer interaction across the school day. Tony's SLP videotaped portions of his day so that she and Tony could examine his behavior, body language (his and others), turn taking, eye contact (his and others), distance, and positioning during their social interaction and similar components of the social and communicative situation. By having the video, the SLP can point out to Tony exactly what he and others are doing, what needs to be copied, changed, and so forth.

To allow for further flexibility of the learning experience, Tony's SLP collected digital video of social situations in and out of the classroom. With the assistance of iMovie (see http://www.apple.com), his SLP edited the video and audio to incorporate learning experiences for Tony. For example, to illustrate turn taking, Tony's SLP edited the video to compare what he was doing to an appropriate model. They developed this into a 30-second clip, burned it to a CD-ROM and now Tony, his teachers, paraprofessionals, and SLP have easy and immediate access to the clip for practice purposes. Apple's iMovie is one of several digital video editing applications that are increasingly available to adults and even children.

Organization Skills

Teachers often complain about students' inability to focus and maintain the necessary concentration to comprehend the subject material. For some students with AS, the same teachers might offer concern about a unique ability to hyper-focus. That is, many students with AS will hyper-focus on a task, losing all sense of time in the meantime. As a result, these students focus on one task for too long, are often chronically late, and are often unprepared for the subsequent task because their focus challenged their time to collect thoughts and gather needed materials.

Technology solutions that can assist students who hyper-focus include a variety of clock options that make them aware of the passage of time, prompt them to move on to another task, and basically make them more aware of the passage of time. For example, the Visual Timer (see http://www.integrationscatalog.com/products/visual_timer.jsp) gives instant feedback on the amount of time left for an activity. The clock relies heavily on a visual system for sequencing and preparing for classroom transitions. Similarly, an increasing number of digital wrist watches offer time prompts and reminders to assist users in keeping track of time. Most offer audio output reminders; however, discreet pulse or vibration prompts are preferred for students working in the general education setting. For an entire class, clocks developed for those with visual impairments can be a wonderful solution. These talking clocks (see http://www.maxiaids.com) can be programmed with the student's voice or related sounds to prompt students at any time that would allow the student to prepare for an upcoming transition.

Many students with AS demonstrate impulsive behaviors that impact their ability to follow directions, maintain focus, and provide structure and organization to their immediate environment. Awareness, control, and self-monitoring of these behaviors is particularly difficult. To address impulsivity and assist the student and the classroom teacher, several interventions appear promising, including PDAs which have increasingly been used to address the needs of these children.

PDAs are becoming prevalent in daily life. They offer a variety of features that make them more user friendly than traditional desktop systems, including touch-screen interfaces (that replace mouse and keyboard use), built-in audio recording, playback capacity, and so forth. In addition, their portability provides the potential for powerful, computer-aided assistance in a wide variety of community settings, and the use of mainstream hardware platforms has the potential to keep costs lower than the high-priced dedicated assistive technology hardware devices.

PDAs also offer a small, compact, and easy-to-use way to allow students to monitor impulsive behaviors while structuring their environment and learning day. Used with students with other disabilities (i.e., mental retardation, learning disabilities, attention deficit disorder), PDAs have been reported to be an effective instructional and support tool (Davies, Stock, & Wehmeyer, 2002). A recent study with a student with AS (Jones, Myles, Gagnon, & Hagiwara, 2004) found that with the assistance of a PDA, inappropriate commenting, blurting, and questioning was decreased. PDAs have also been used to assist students with AS record and complete homework (Myles, Ferguson, & Hagiwara, in press) and complete routines at home (Ferguson, Myles, & Hagiwara, in press).

While the PDA offers a compatible, easy-to-use tool for many students with AS, other assistive technology devices can also help students organize and self-monitor their actions. Often referred to as portable word processors, devices like the AlphaSmart (see http://www.alphasmart .com/) are increasingly being purchased and used by school districts. The AlphaSmart (e.g., AlphaSmart 3000) allows students to enter and edit text and send it to any computer for formatting or directly to a printer. Its portability allows students to use it anywhere and anytime—in the classroom, at home, or on field trips. The Dana Wireless extends the word processing function by featuring Palm components, allowing the student to use the portable device as a word processor as well as a scheduler, organizer, and reminder. In addition, the wireless feature enables the user to "beam" information to printers and other capable devices, thus eliminating the need for additional paper or lost assignments. Similar portable word processors include QuickPad (see http://www.quickpad.com) and Dreamwriter (see http://www.dreamwriter.com/), both offering a portable, easy-to-use, and inexpensive word processor.

Classroom Instruction

Many students with AS need academic modifications that enable them to succeed in the general education classroom. Whether for structuring daily routines, priming for transitions, or assistance in transitions from class to class, students with AS can benefit from reasonable modifications and accommodations. Technology can aid students with a variety of tasks, including note taking and completing assignments.

Note Taking

In a majority of classrooms, note taking skills are required and expected to assist the learning process. For many students with AS, motor problems preclude getting important content onto the paper. Fortunately, electronic text offers multiple options and flexible solutions.

For example, to address note taking concerns, teachers should develop their lecture notes via a word processing program like Microsoft Word (see http://www.microsoft.com). Here the teacher can organize his thoughts while also developing outlines, concept maps, content organizers, and similar study tools by simply manipulating electronic notes. Literally with the click of a mouse, teachers can provide study sheets, lesson outlines, practice worksheets, and similar material to assist students who have limited note taking abilities.

As mentioned, hand held devices (e.g., PDAs) and portable word processors can also assist students in taking notes, organizing concepts, and accessing information. Some teachers even "beam" information from their personal PDA to a student's PDA, allowing for notes and study guides to be shared without transferring paper (see http://www.palm.com).

Writing

Motor problems and organizational issues often challenge the writing process for students with AS. As students begin to write, they often associate sounds with the shapes of words and letters, then look to see if the words make sense and are spelled correctly. They read what they have written to themselves or aloud. When composing or revising, they look to previous sections and insert, erase, reorganize, or make notes. Pens and pencils are their writing tools; legibility in written work is important. To address potential problems in this area, word processors can enhance student writing abilities by offering alternative strategies to production and learning.

Students with disabilities frequently require alternative ways of creating written text. A continuum of writing tools and strategies includes pencils to computers to voice input. While low-tech options should be considered, computers offer a variety of features that can support the writing process. For example, using a keyboard to write often eliminates legibility issues. Computers can also provide assistance with visual organization, outlining, and step-by-step direction following—all which support the writing process.

The most easily available classroom technology is word processing programs (e.g., Microsoft Word), which are used to create and work with text or words, such as in writing spelling lists, letters, reports, compositions, or assignments. These programs, basic to classroom computer use, include several common features to make writing easier and more fun for students. For example, with the click of a mouse, students can change the appearance of the text (e.g., color, font, text size, highlight), which in turn can add emphasis or purpose to text on a page or the screen.

Microsoft Word and other word processing programs can also be customized to meet student needs. That is, a number of automatic options can be used that address frequent uses and needs. For instance, the "auto text" option allows the student to insert frequently used text and graphics (e.g., headings, words, names, addresses) when he or she types a few identifying characters. The "auto correct" option programs the word processor to automatically correct certain misspelled words as they are typed (e.g., studnet = student), allowing the student to become more efficient in her work. More important for young learners, a list of vocabulary can be included to assist in the writing process.

Writing Aids

In conjunction with the word processor, software is increasingly being developed to help students increase vocabulary, correct spelling, and ease the writing process. For example, *Kidspiration, Inspiration,* and *Draft Builder* assist learners in generating and organizing thoughts they wish to convey in writing. While word processors have internal spell checks, handheld devices like the Franklin Spelling Tool (see http://www. franklin.com) are increasing in use due to low cost, portability, and multiple uses.

Talking Word Processors

Increasingly, manufacturers are developing and schools are using talking word processing programs that can help introduce writing to students. These programs speak aloud what is typed into the computer; they can echo each letter as it is typed and each word as the spacebar is pressed, or they can read an entire sentence, including punctuation, once a student has completed a thought. When beginning to write, most students find they benefit from visual and auditory supports. The ability to hear a letter or word spoken as it is typed helps children to more quickly associate letters and words with their sounds, thereby connecting visual and auditory images of words. While many word processors include audio output features, popular talking word processors include Write Outloud (see http://www.donjohnston.com), IntelliTalk II (see http://www.intelli tools.com), and eReader (see http://www.cast.org).

Word Prediction

As mentioned above, basic word processors can be formatted to offer word prediction options for young learners as well as those with writing or learning difficulties. For students who know what they want to write but have difficulty forming the words or thinking of new words to use, word prediction programs are used with word processors to provide a more efficient way of producing written work. Thus a novice writer can create a complete word by typing one or two letters. The programs reduce the number of keystrokes made by "predicting" the desired word after a student types a single letter. Some programs even include a "predict ahead" feature that anticipates the next word. These programs can effectively improve the quality and level of writing by suggesting new words stored in a customizable dictionary. Popular word prediction programs include Co-Writer 400 (see http://www.donjohnston.com), EZ Keys (see http://www.words-plus.com), Gus! Word Prediction (see http://www.gus inc.com), and Word Q (see http://www.wordq.com).

Audio Input and Speech Recognition

Speech recognition software provides an alternative to help students to write more efficiently. With speech recognition software and computer hardware, a student trains the computer to recognize his voice for writing or giving computer commands. Students can use voice recognition to write in a word processor or to create an e-mail message. It can also execute program commands, such as saving or printing, or control the mouse.

Speech recognition is a rapidly growing and changing technology field. Many companies offer various options (e.g., Dragon Naturally Speaking Standard at http://www.dragonsys.com). As you investigate these programs look for features that are most beneficial for individual students.

- Continuous speech. A student speaks a string of words with a normal rate of speech, not pausing between words.
- Dedicated word processor. A built-in word processor provides the user a quick start.
- Hands-free. A student's voice can create text, input commands, and perform mouse movements. Other programs require using the keyboard and mouse together with the student's speech.
- Playback. The spoken text is repeated in the student's voice.
- Text-to-speech. The produced text is read back with a computer voice. This may make it easier to identify errors.
- Use across applications. Some programs work with one or two applications, such as word processors. Others work with all software programs.
- Customization. A variety of options should be examined, including:

  1. Built-in keyboard commands
  2. Built-in voice navigation

Alternative Textbooks

Considering that 80–85% of what we teach in the middle and secondary general education classroom is based on what a student reads, alternative ways to access reading materials are critical for students who have reading difficulties. For many students with AS, this is not so much a reading issue as it is an organizational issue. Thus it is critical that students with AS receive assistance in organizing material as well as identifying and separating critical information (e.g., main ideas) from the rest of the text. For example, for some students, the use of timelines, visual organizers, concept maps, and chapter outlines is critical to a complete comprehension of the reading material.

Fortunately, with the advent of electronic text, more and more options are becoming available for students to increase their reading abilities and organize the text they are required to read. For all learners, books on tape represent an option that is becoming increasingly available through textbook manufacturers, local libraries, and organizations for the visually impaired (see http://www.clb.org). An increasing number of books are also available via CD-ROM and the Internet for immediate download (see http://www.bartleby.com). Contact the publishing company supplying the classroom textbook as many provide electronic options for teachers, students, and parents (see http://www.hmco.com). Some publishers are actually examining ways to provide the entire textbook via an interactive Web site (see http://www.ignitelearning.com/index.shtml).

SUMMARY

The overview offered in this chapter merely presents the "tip of the iceberg" in possible technology solutions for students with AS. It is critical that parents and teachers work together to identify the specific needs of the learner, examine the environmental constraints and demands, and then look to technology solutions. If technology solutions are considered as a team, then appropriate tools or devices can be found to address the issues challenging the student in the classroom.

Making Each Year Successful: Issues in Transition

7

by Ronda L. Schelvan,
Terri Cooper Swanson, and Sheila M. Smith

When working with students with AS and other disabilities, the term *transition* is used two ways. First, *transition* refers to the movement of students in between activities and environments. Second, *transition* is also used to describe the process of supporting students as they move from school to the community following graduation from high school. This chapter highlights the importance of both types of transition: (a) planning transitions for students with AS throughout their school day, as well as (b) the *Individuals with Disabilities Education Act* (IDEA) requirements, which educators must follow when planning transitions between grade levels, changes in levels of service, and when planning for accessing transition services after high school.

CASE STUDY: JACK

Jack, a first grader with AS, can usually follow the class routine when his teacher, Mrs. Johnson, is there. When Mrs. Johnson is there the schedule stays the same. Today, Mr. Moore is substituting. It is 9:00 a.m.; everyone knows that it is time for math. Mr. Moore told everyone to get their spelling books. This made Jack mad. Jack refused to get out his spelling book.

TRANSITIONING BETWEEN ACTIVITIES AND ENVIRONMENTS

Students with AS typically have trouble changing activities and settings, beginning a new school year, transitioning to a new school, moving from elementary to secondary school environments, and transitioning from school to adult environments. They also have difficulty coping with social and academic expectations and the hidden curriculum of various settings. The purpose of transition planning is to reduce the stress and anxiety change brings to students with AS, while allowing them opportunities to be successful.

Transition means much more than simply changing activities or environments. For students with AS, transitions are a multilayered, ongoing process that involves socialization, communication, and behavior—three major areas of impairment for this group of individuals. It is important to remember that even for typically developing students, change can be frustrating and challenging. For students with AS, imagine how difficult and stressful coping with change can be. Evidence suggests that the areas of behavior and socialization continue to be of greatest concern for students with AS, especially as they move into the secondary school setting (Klin et al., 2000).

School settings have a structure for academic learning, yet most peer interaction and socializing occurs during unstructured times and settings. This poses major challenges on several fronts for students with AS, who need structure and predictability throughout their day, especially during the unstructured times such as lunch, recess, bus rides, and passing times between classes. Transition planning allows teachers to prepare educational interventions that anticipate situations rather than react after something has occurred. Transition planning is a proactive rather than a reactive process (Marks et al., 2003).

An adaptation of the *Students' Multiple Worlds Model* (Phelan, Yu, & Davidson, 1994) visually depicts the complexity and interdependency of relationships involved with transitions (see Figure 7.1). As illustrated, transitions involve social interactions, social reciprocity, organizing, planning, shifting attention, and multitasking, all difficult areas for students with AS. Thus transition planning is of the utmost importance.

Understanding roles and strategies plays an important part in the transition process. For children and youth with AS, this is a challenge because of their characteristics. That is, lack of flexibility, misunderstandings of the perceptions of others, challenges understanding and engaging in social interactions, as well as an inability to understand the hidden curriculum can make transitions between environments difficult. While

Figure 7.1   Students' Multiple Worlds Model

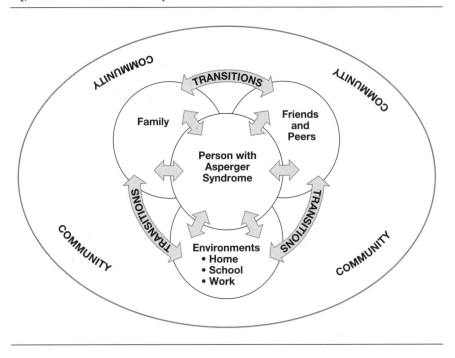

everyone has his or her own set of inclinations and challenges, students with AS present with unique traits that often make transitions stressful. For example, family, friends, as well as home, school, work, and community have their own set of expectations for any individual, and particularly for students with AS. Peers of students with AS expect them to have similar interests, likes or dislikes, and views. When children and youth with AS do not share these aspects with peers, it is often difficult for friendships or satisfying peer relationships to develop. Table 7.1 overviews the inclinations and expectations that various individuals have for students with AS and the challenges apparent in AS that make meeting these expectations difficult.

Effective transition planning involves many stakeholders. It takes a team to ensure smooth, successful transitions. Although at times difficult, the transition process should not be overwhelming. Proactive planning can yield practical strategies for educators such as background knowledge of the student, how to use the student's special interests to instruct and motivate him or her, as well as meeting the social-emotional, behavioral, and educational needs of students with AS. *Proactive* is a key word—teams must plan ahead.

The transition process takes time, collaboration, and effort and must be in place before a student changes environments. Transition planning is not only about structuring the environment to ensure success—it also entails teaching students with AS the compensatory skills they need to

Table 7.1   Traits of Students With AS That May Impact Transition

Roles	Inclinations	Challenges
Person with AS	• Innocent, naïve • Narrow, focused intense "special interests" • Concrete, literal thinkers • Visual learners • Moral sense of right and wrong	• Lack of organizational skills • Difficulty with emotions • High stress and anxiety • Lack of social reciprocity • Inability to carry on conversations
Family	• Expectations of and for each family member • Culture (ethnic and/ or religious) • Belief systems • Socio-economic values	• Lack of understanding • Sibling rivalry • Stress, anxiety, depression • Unequal responsibilities • Miscommunication
Friends and peers	• Similar interests • Shared beliefs • Common goals • Likes/dislikes	• Lack of understanding • Peer pressure • Lack of acceptance • Lack of common interests
Environments • Home • School • Work	• Rules • Expectations • Performance • Perceptions	• Inability to perform • Hidden curriculum • Unspoken rules • Lack of empathy
Community	• Value system • Laws • Cultures • Resources • Perceptions	• Lack of funding • Loss of jobs • Misconceptions • Moral standards

become self-advocates. It is important to involve students to the best of their abilities in transition planning. In addition, when transition services are being discussed students must be invited to team meetings, and if they cannot attend, their interests and preferences must be represented (Martin, 2002) (see Table 7.2).

This chapter discusses the importance of building self-awareness, self-esteem, and self-determination in students with AS; general strategies to consider when planning daily transitions; ways to ensure success through transition planning; and ideas for creating a personal file to share information from year to year. The section titled Self-Concept and Transitions provides the reader with an understanding of the importance of building self-esteem along with strategies for increasing self-concept. General Strategies for Successful Daily Transitions includes a checklist of basic supports which should be in place to ensure smooth, ongoing transitions. Individualized Education Plan/Transition Planning Meetings addresses the importance of a team approach when planning supports for new environments; Creating a

Table 7.2   Transition Processes and Planning

Transition Processes Should:	*Transition Planning Should:*
<ul><li>Be individualized, child-specific</li><li>Anticipate each child's development to address the ever-changing academic, social-emotional, and physical needs</li><li>Consider each child as an active, productive learner</li><li>Foster positive relationships among the participants (children, families, and educators)</li><li>Be based on mutual trust and respect</li><li>Be sensitive to family and community strengths and needs</li><li>Identify and implement the necessary supports (staff, materials, orientation, and training)</li><li>Observe all environments, making accommodations and modifications as necessary</li><li>Be proactive, well planned, flexible</li><li>Include long-term goal setting versus short-term orientation</li><li>Be evaluated and assessed regularly</li></ul>	<ul><li>Reduce stress and anxiety in a student with AS, his family, and educators</li><li>Decrease frustration</li><li>Ease participation in classroom activities and routines</li><li>Increase self-esteem, self-respect, self-determination</li><li>Lessen chance of disruptive behaviors</li><li>Improve attention to task</li></ul>

Personal File provides an example of how to share important information from year to year. Finally, Planning for Transition Services provides the information needed to prepare for adult life after graduation.

SELF-CONCEPT AND TRANSITIONS

Because social impairment is one of the core characteristics of AS, it is imperative not to underestimate the importance of the use of social skills in transitioning. Students with AS tend to be more immature than their peers and often develop a negative self-concept. At times, they develop a poor attitude about themselves or others, which makes it difficult for them to attempt social interactions (Kransy, Williams, Provencal, & Ozonoff, 2003). As shown in Figure 7.2, self-concept is the heart of socialization, and the ability to understand social aspects is a key part of transitions.

Think of a student's self-concept as a spring, with self-awareness (understanding one's feelings and emotions; knowing who one is), self-esteem (comprehending how one feels about oneself), and self-determination (having the opportunity and being able to make personal choices and decisions about daily life) as the coils. When everything is in alignment the coils are flexible—they can bend under pressure, bounce back, and handle stress. Creating positive self-awareness builds positive self-esteem, which leads to focused self-determination, which increases self-awareness, builds self-esteem, leads to self-determination, and so on (see Figure 7.3).

Figure 7.2 Self–Concept Is the Heart of Socialization

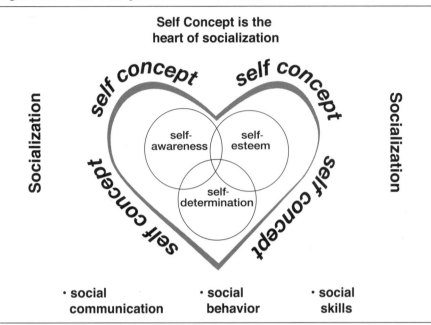

Figure 7.3 Creating Positive Self–Awareness

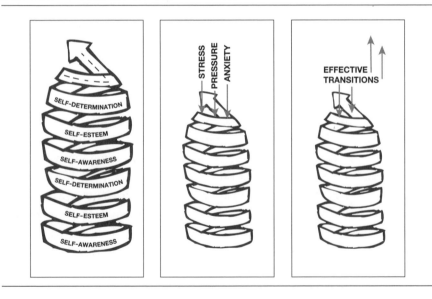

Tanisha, a fifth grader with AS, lacks an understanding of her emotions and often expresses disappointment with anger (limited self-awareness). She will verbalize her low self-esteem by focusing on negative self-talk ("I am dumb, I cannot do this"). Although she has been encouraged to make choices, her self-determination skills are minimal. Tanisha's "self-concept coil" is out of alignment. She will have difficulty being flexible. When she becomes stressed, she will not be able to "bounce back" without an additional support.

Dessmone, a typical fifth grader, has a solid understanding of her feelings and emotions (self-awareness). She is able to express them in appropriate ways. She feels good about herself and is building positive self-esteem. Her self-determination is strengthened through structured choice making in all environments. Dessmone's "self-concept coil" is in alignment. When faced with stressful or challenging situations she will feel anxious, yet has the ability to flex, bend, and regroup with minimal support.

Similar to their typically developing peers, children with AS want to "fit in." When they enter school, the primary social-behavioral adjustments are adaptive classroom behavior and interpersonal competence. By second or third grade, most children with AS begin to realize their differences. This increase in self-awareness often leads to poor self-concept, which can turn into depression, especially as students enter junior high and high school where social pressures and overall demands increase (Moyes, 2001). Three components of self-concept (self-awareness, self-esteem, and self-determination) play an important part in transitions and life success for children and youth with AS. Table 7.3 gives an overview of simple strategies that can result in increased self-concept.

Ian, a boy with AS, and Jason had been friends since kindergarten. Both boys loved trains. Now that they are in third grade, Jason is beginning to have different interests, and Ian often feels left out. They got into an argument on the playground when Jason wanted to play kick ball with the other boys. Ian yelled that he did not want to be Jason's friend anymore because he did not want to play trains. Ian spent the rest of recess doing what appeared to be taunting Jason. During the next recess, Ian refused to go outside. Instead, he remained in his seat repeating that he did not have any friends because no one liked him and since no one liked him, he should not have to go outside. Ian did not understand how to identify and share his feelings of disappointment and frustration. He was also not aware of keeping his distance (personal space). Assisting students with AS, like Ian, in building their self-concept should also include learning self-control and self-management strategies, especially in the area of friendships. Techniques mentioned in previous chapters, such as social skills training and Circle of Friends, are valuable when incorporated in transition plans.

GENERAL STRATEGIES FOR SUCCESSFUL DAILY TRANSITIONS

Daily transitions are those that occur as the student moves from one activity or environment to another. These transitions are an ongoing concern

Table 7.3   Examples of Ways to Build Self-Concept

SELF-CONCEPT VARIABLE	

Self-awareness	• Feelings and emotions:
	  • Teach students to identify and label their feelings and emotions.
	  • Teach them to recognize and read emotions in others, including body language, nonverbal communication, and facial expressions. Teach imagination and pretending skills (reality versus make-believe).
	• Personal space:
	  • Make them aware of their proximity to others.
	  • Help them create a visual example of their own space.

Self-esteem	• Encourage positive self-talk such as:
	  • I can do _____.
	  • I am really good at _____.
	  • I care about _____.
	• Use their special interests as tools in the classroom. Peers will look up to them and learn to value their talents.
	• Use special interests as motivators.

Self-determination	• Offer and encourage choice making (simple and complex). • Demonstrate how to turn mistakes into learning opportunities. • Promote self-reflection, self-evaluation. • Encourage participation in their own IEP development. • Role play ways to speak up for themselves (self-advocacy).

for students with AS; therefore, planning for daily transitions must be an ongoing process. Students need to know what to do as well as what not to do, what to expect, when an activity will be finished, and what they are supposed to do afterwards. Students with AS also need predictability and routine built into their day. Most resistance from individuals with AS comes from failure to understand rather than noncompliance. Being aware of the student's level of stress and anxiety will help anticipate the amount of support needed to successfully complete daily transitions.

In the case study at the beginning of the chapter, Jack did not understand that the schedule could change, as the class always had math at 9:00 a.m. By providing a daily schedule (visual support), Jack may have been able to better understand and predict the change, therefore transitioning to a new activity with less resistance. If a student requires support in transitioning throughout his or her school day, the specific type of support needed by the student should be included in the IEP. Table 7.4 provides a checklist of basic supports that should always be in place to ensure success during transitions (as discussed in previous chapters).

Table 7.4   Daily Transition Checklist

Daily Transition Checklist for:	Date:

- Predictability of actions and routines
- Visual Supports
  - Visual daily schedules
  - Visual schedule
  - Graphic organizers
  - Signals and cues
  - Contracts
  - Models
  - Maps
  - Written assignment sheets/lists/timelines of task completion
  - Sensory adaptations (hand fidgets, weighted backpack, etc.)

- Easily understood choices
- Clearly defined expectations
- Extra processing time
- Concrete instructions (less verbal, more visual/written)
- Other, as determined by the needs of this individual:

TRANSITION TO ADULTHOOD

CASE STUDY: MIKHAIL

Mikhail is a fifth grader with AS. He is preparing for the transition to the sixth grade in the fall. Mikhail has sensitive hearing and is aware of all of the sounds taking place in the classroom, people talking at the far end of the hallway, and even the sound of writing on the dry erase board in the next classroom. His sensitive hearing makes it extremely difficult for him to focus on his teacher's instructions, and therefore makes assignments difficult to complete because he is not able to fully understand the directions. When Mikhail's schedule changes, he becomes frustrated and at times may cry. The other students find his behavior odd, especially when the schedule change is something fun like an assembly instead of math. He also finds it difficult when the furniture in the classroom is moved or rearranged. His current teacher likes to move the desks and furniture around every few weeks; this frustrates Mikhail. He becomes confused, doesn't know where to find his desk or supplies for class, and becomes overwhelmed and disoriented. When he finally learns where everything is located the teacher moves the room around again. When it is time for recess, or on days when gym class is held outside, Mikhail likes to stay inside and play chess or help one of the paraprofessionals deliver the school mail. When Mikhail first started school, his teacher insisted that he participate in outside recess. When it was warm outside Mikhail didn't seem to mind participating. He would usually bring a book to read or swing on the swings. When the weather turns colder, Mikhail does not like the way his body feels and refuses to go outside. He says that when he gets goose bumps on his body he feels like he is getting pricked with thousands of little needles. This year, as sixth graders, the students are expected to participate in Outdoor School for one week in October. Members of his IEP team are concerned about Mikhail's ability to participate in Outdoor School. The state mandates completion of particular requirements and the level of accommodations that Mikhail requires. Many of Mikhail's teachers are finding that the general education curriculum is not interesting to him, and therefore he is not motivated to learn. Mikhail's IEP team is concerned that if they do not find some way to motivate him he will fail the sixth grade. His parents and Mr. Kernan, his current homeroom teacher, are looking for ways to incorporate Mikhail's special interests into the curriculum, hoping to increase his motivation for completing his academic assignments (see Chapter 3 for information on using special interests). Mikhail also has difficulty with his handwriting. Often Mikhail will refuse to complete assignments independently if he has to do a lot of writing. Mrs. Keith, the technology specialist, is looking into assistive technology to help him complete writing assignments independently (see Chapter 6 for information on assistive technology).

INDIVIDUALIZED EDUCATION PLAN/ TRANSITION PLANNING MEETINGS

A transition planning meeting is a time for everyone involved to begin identifying the supports a student needs and to discuss ways to ensure they are implemented before a major transition happens (i.e., beginning a new school year, transitioning to a new school, or moving from elementary to secondary school environments). It is important for representatives from each environment to be present. For example, when a student is moving from middle to high school, teachers from both schools should attend the transition planning meeting. Designate someone to take notes and someone to be the timekeeper to maintain the group's focus. After the meeting, everyone present should receive a copy of the notes. In addition, notes from transition planning meetings should be kept in the student's file, to assist teams in creating an effective timeline and allow for reference as needed. A sample note-keeping form appears in Figure 7.4.

Mikhail's IEP team will meet in April to begin planning for next year's transition. The note-keeping form serves as an agenda as well as a record. Team members list three or four items to be discussed, then prioritize these items. As the discussion takes place, a note keeper records the key points, making note of any needed follow-up including target dates for item completion. Before the meeting is adjourned, a future meeting date is determined. Everyone receives a copy of the notes, ensuring accountability for the transition process.

Because of the special needs of children and youth with AS, myriad concerns must be addressed when planning transitions. The sample transition checklist in Figure 7.5 encompasses some of the considerations for transitioning students entering middle school through students leaving the school system to join the workforce or enter higher education.

(Text continues on page 144)

Figure 7.4   Sample Agenda/Record Keeping Form

Student: Mikhail B.   Date: _____ April 18

Team Members Present: Dorey Smith, Ron Kamanuii, Johanna Washington, Carlos Pedras, Javen Ming, Maya Hagiwara, Marcia Tims, Monica Green, Arlene Page, and Sally Roseberg

Agenda Items (list items then rank in prioritized order)	Purpose of This Meeting:	Follow-Up	By Who?	By When?
	Begin looking at Mikhail's transition needs from 5th to 6th grade.			
	Discussion:			
3 Outdoor school?	1. *Next year's home room teacher.* Staff assignments have not been decided yet, but Mikhail needs a teacher who has a structured class environment, is flexible when it comes to his distracting sounds, and has a sense of humor. Mrs. Z would be a good match if she is still teaching 6th grade.	1. Check to see when staff assignments will be made, let people know before next meeting to allow time for brainstorming.	Ron	April 25
1 Next year's homeroom teacher?	2. *Staff training.* Which staff have had training? What type of training is needed? *FYI.* All-staff inservice on sensory awareness is scheduled for sometime in May.	2. Ask for staff input on training needs (info survey?)	Javen	April 29
4 Curriculum modifications		3. Talk with 6th-grade teachers at separate meeting to discuss all that is involved.	Arlene will schedule.	By the middle of May
2 Staff training	3. *Outdoor school.* Scheduled for October 10-14. What supports will Mikhail need to be successful? Team needs to start thinking now because it will come fast once school starts in the fall.	4. Begin to compare Mikhail's IEP goals to curriculum. Look at strategies, accommodations, assistive technology, etc.	Sally	April 29
	4. *Curriculum modifications.* What is needed? Who will do them?			
	5. *Assessment.* Are any assessments needed?			

Date of next meeting: *Tuesday, April 29 at 3:00 p.m.*

Place of next meeting: Mr. K's Room 24

Figure 7.5   Transition Checklist

ACADEMIC MODIFICATIONS

Priming

❑ Determine whether priming will help meet the student's need for predictability.
    ❑ Analyze student needs and classroom demands to determine which classes will require priming.
    ❑ Identify who will prime.
    ❑ Designate whether priming will use actual or similar materials.
    ❑ Determine where and when priming will occur.

Classroom Assignments

❑ Determine the student's needs concerning assignments.
    ❑ Provide the student with extra time to complete assignments.
    ❑ Shorten the length of assignments.
    ❑ Reduce the number of assignments.
    ❑ Break assignments into smaller segments.
    ❑ Provide samples/models of completed assignments and/or a list of specific criteria.
    ❑ Allow the student to use the computer for schoolwork and/or homework.
    ❑ Allow the student to demonstrate mastery of concepts through alternate means.

Note Taking

❑ Indicate the type of note taking supports needed by the student.
    ❑ Provide a complete outline.
    ❑ Give student a skeletal outline.
    ❑ Identify a peer who can take notes for the student.
    ❑ Allow student to use outlining software.

Graphic Organizers

❑ Determine whether graphic organizers are needed to facilitate skill acquisition and maintenance.
❑ Specify which type of graphic organizers will be needed:
    ❑ Hierarchical
    ❑ Conceptual
    ❑ Sequential
    ❑ Cyclical
    ❑ Other

❑ Determine who will construct and provide organizer to student.
    ❑ Teacher
    ❑ Peer
    ❑ Student with template
    ❑ Student with outlining software

Enrichment

❑ Determine the type of enrichment needed.
    ❑ Specify how the enrichment area will be identified.
    ❑ Determine when and how enrichment will be provided.
    ❑ Decide whether a learning contract with specified working conditions is needed.

Homework

❑ Identify which class subjects will include homework responsibilities.
❑ Determine homework modifications.
    ❑ Present homework assignments visually (on board, etc.) in addition to orally.
    ❑ Provide the student with a homework sheet or planner.

Figure 7.5

    ❑ Provide peer or teacher assistance in recording homework assignments.
    ❑ Provide student with the assignment in written format.
    ❑ Reduce the amount of homework.
    ❑ Provide a study hall period to allow the student time to complete homework at school.
❑ Identify home strategy for completing homework.
    ❑ Designate place and time for homework completion.
    ❑ Define organization to get homework back to school.
    ❑ Name contact if additional clarification is needed on homework.

MODIFICATIONS FOR UNSTRUCTURED OR
LESS STRUCTURED TIMES

Transportation/Bus

❑ Identify who will teach the student the bus routine.
❑ Determine who will provide assistance for the student when the bus arrives at school.
❑ Determine how long assistance will be needed in getting to and from the bus throughout the year.
❑ Identify the peer or school personnel to be assigned to assist the student in this process, also backups.
❑ Provide a pickup or drop-off closer to the student's house.
❑ Provide adult supervision at the bus stop.
❑ Provide a peer "buddy" to wait with the student at the bus stop and sit with the student on the bus.
❑ Provide preferential seating on the bus.
❑ Provide a monitor or aide on the bus.
❑ Arrange for special bus.

Physical Education

❑ Consider whether to exempt the student from PE.
❑ Assign the student a specific role for PE such as score keeper, equipment manager, etc.
❑ Assign teams rather than allow students to choose teams themselves.
❑ Have school personnel monitor, at least twice weekly, the student's perceptions of PE.
❑ Help the student problem-solve difficulties.

Lunch

❑ Have school personnel available during the first week of school to assist the student in navigating the cafeteria line, finding a place to sit, and engaging in an appropriate activity after eating.
❑ Help the student identify school personnel that she can approach when encountering problems.
❑ Have school personnel closely monitor the student's interactions and intervene when problems occur (i.e., during interactions, when stressed or overwhelmed, when experiencing sensory overload).
❑ Have school personnel monitor, at least twice weekly, the student's perceptions of the lunch period.
❑ Help the student problem-solve any difficulties.
❑ Provide assigned seating with a preferred friend, away from problem peers and/or near an adult.
❑ Provide a peer "buddy/buddies" during lunchtime.
❑ Allow student to leave the cafeteria once he has finished eating and/or to engage in a calming activity.
❑ Allow the student to eat lunch in an alternative location if necessary.

(Continued)

Figure 7.5

ChangingClasses

❏ Provide peer or teacher assistance to help the student manage the crowded hallways, open locker, locate the proper materials, and find the correct classroom.
❏ Provide the student with additional time for class changes.
❏ Allow alternate passing time when the hallways are free from other students.

Changes in Routine

❏ Specify whether the student needs to be informed of any changes in typical classroom procedures
❏ Determine what additional supports the student needs when changes occur.

Before and After School

1. Identify when the student should arrive at school.
2. Determine whether a specific room should be used during this time.
3. Identify peers to support the student at this time.
4. Provide structured activities.

ENVIRONMENTAL SUPPORTS

Preferential Seating

❏ Determine if preferential seating is necessary.
   ❏ Identify location.
   ❏ Identify peers who can support student.

Organizational Strategies

❏ Determine the student's needs concerning organization of papers and materials.
❏ Provide assistance in organizing the backpack, locker, and/or desk and teach the student to do these.
❏ Teach the student to use timelines.
❏ Instruct the student on how to develop a to-do list.
❏ Other (specify).

Home Base

❏ Identify when home base will be used.
   ❏ Before school or early morning
   ❏ Following specific classes
   ❏ At the end of the day

❏ Determine cue to prompt home base.
❏ Determine home base location.
❏ Identify activities that will occur during home base.

Visual Supports

❏ Identify which supports are needed.
   ❏ Map of school outlining classes
   ❏ List of classes, room numbers, books and other supplies
   ❏ List of teacher expectations and routines for each class
   ❏ Outlines and notes from lectures
   ❏ Model of assignments

(Continued)

Figure 7.5

    ❑ Test reminders
    ❑ Schedule changes
    ❑ Cue to home base
    ❑ Other (specify)
    ❑ Visual schedule

SOCIAL SUPPORTS

Hidden Curriculum

❑ Identify hidden curriculum items.
❑ Define who will teach hidden curriculum.
❑ Determine when instruction will occur.

Circle of Friends

❑ Provide awareness training to peers.
❑ Identify peers to participate in Circle of Friends.
❑ Determine when Circle of Friends is needed to support student.

Social Skills Instruction

❑ Determine need for direct instruction.
    ❑ Identify curriculum and instructor.
    ❑ Determine when social skills instruction will occur.

❑ Determine if acting lessons may support social skills instruction.
    ❑ Identify coach's need for AS awareness training.
    ❑ Provide awareness training to other student actors.

❑ Consider whether social stories are a viable means of instruction.
    ❑ Identify individual who can create social narratives
    ❑ Determine how the need for a social narrative will be communicated.
    ❑ Determine who will monitor social narrative effectiveness.

Social Skills Interpretation

❑ Determine social skills interpreter.
❑ Ensure social skills interpreter knows how to use (a) cartooning, (b) social autopsies, (c) SOCCSS and (d) sensory awareness.
❑ Identify when student will have access to the social skills interpreter.
    ❑ Scheduled time as needed

From *Asperger Syndrome and Adolescence: Practical Solutions for School Success,* by B. S. Myles and D. Andreon (2001). Reprinted with permission from Autism Asperger Publishing Company, Shawnee Mission, KS.

Table 7.5 Transition Considerations

Setting	Environment	Social-Emotional	Academic	Behavioral
Pre-K	❑ Natural setting, includes similar-age peers, who are both social and verbal ❑ Visually structured ❑ Clear, defined boundaries ❑ Designated quiet area to reduce anxiety and sensory overload	❑ Curriculum addresses the core deficits of students with AS ❑ Foster self-awareness of feelings and emotions ❑ Encourage friendships and develop positive play skills	❑ Schedule reflects balanced variety of activities that address the functional needs and skills of the student both cognitively and adaptively ❑ Use student's special interests to enhance learning	❑ Staff and classroom expectations meet student's needs ❑ Reduce stress and anxiety ❑ Build in choice making throughout the day
❑ Make sure staff is trained in AS ❑ Use an integrated approach for goals and services ❑ Teach generalization skills ❑ Focus on the positive ❑ Be proactive				
Elementary	Same as Pre-K plus: ❑ Consider student needs with teacher style ❑ Use visual supports, graphic organizers ❑ Provide structure to unstructured activities	Same as Pre-K plus: ❑ Build self-esteem ❑ Use Circle of Friends and social skills groups to build relationships ❑ Teach the concept of home base and safe person ❑ Allow and encourage student to be a leader/helper	Same as Pre-K plus: ❑ Be respectful of learner's strengths and challenges ❑ Modify and adjust academic expectations to meet student capabilities ❑ Introduce concept of leisure skills	Same as Pre-K plus: ❑ Make sure positive behavioral supports are in place ❑ Recognize communication of behaviors ❑ Be aware of teaching independence instead of learned helplessness
Same as Pre-K plus: ❑ Conduct and review assessments ❑ Check for understanding				

(Continued)

Table 7.5 (Continued)

Setting	Environment	Social-Emotional	Academic	Behavioral
Middle	Same as elementary plus: ❑ Watch for bullying ❑ Be sensitive to possibility of depression	Same as elementary plus: ❑ Provide orientation ❑ Practice routines ❑ Provide maps and written directions	Same as elementary plus: ❑ Analyze effect of stress and anxiety ❑ Teach self-reflection, self-evaluation ❑ Expand vocabulary of emotions/feelings ❑ Change the format of social skills training	Same as elementary plus: ❑ Build in homework strategies/modifications ❑ Provide study hall ❑ Provide opportunities for leadership in special interest areas ❑ Further define leisure skills	Same as elementary plus: ❑ Honor and value student's opinions ❑ Reassess motivation and reinforcements ❑ Teach the hidden curriculum ❑ Introduce self-determination curriculum ❑ Establish understanding of the roles and responsibility of law enforcement
High School	Same as middle plus: ❑ Watch for intimidation and harassment	Same as middle plus: ❑ Provide orientation opportunities prior to beginning of the year ❑ Possibly attend a summer class	Same as middle plus: ❑ Provide work experience ❑ Continue to encourage friendships/ relationships, build on like interests	Same as middle plus: ❑ Provide enrichment activities in addition to academics	Same as middle plus: ❑ Encourage and support self-advocacy
School to Work	Same as high school	Same as high school plus: ❑ Change from high school setting to college or work setting	Same as high school plus: ❑ Expand friendships to the next environment	Same as high school plus: ❑ Focus continues to be academics or transfers to work environment	Same as high school plus: ❑ Builds on self-determination and self-advocacy

From *Asperger Syndrome and Adolescence: Practical Solutions for School Success*, by B. S. Myles and D. Andreon (2001). Reprinted with permission from Autism Asperger Publishing Company, Shawnee Mission, KS.

CASE STUDY: CONNIE

Connie, an eighth grader with AS, has always had difficulty when asked to work in small, cooperative learning groups. Information in her personal file reflects the difficulty from two teacher's perspectives.

Mrs. Casper writes, "Connie is stubborn and willful. She refuses to participate in small group activities, choosing instead to do her own thing rather than help the others complete the project."

Mr. Torres writes, "Connie can focus on her work when working individually or with a group of three or fewer students. She can also focus on the task when she is given specific step-by-step, written directions."

CREATING A PERSONAL FILE

Creating a personal file for a student with AS adds a positive approach to easing transitions from year to year. A personal file is a *confidential* collection of information specific to the student that is passed on from year to year. It is different from a cumulative file in that it allows a receiving teacher to gain pertinent information regarding the student's strengths and challenges in addition to the usual testing data and report card grades. Information should *always* be written in positive, observable terms so as not to bias another person's impressions of the student. In the case study, Mrs. Casper states an opinion, whereas Mr. Torres uses positive, observable terms, which give a clearer picture of Connie's needs. Mr. Torres is able to provide useful information that can transition with Connie. The personal file should be brightly colored and labeled with the student's name so it is easily recognized. Since the information in the folder is confidential, it should be marked as such. The folder might include the following information:

1. A *Personal File Inventory* is a list of key components which, at a glance, let the teacher know what is included in the student's personal file. All of the information should be cumulative and updated at least annually. The file should become a comprehensive overview of the student's strengths, challenges, and educational program (see Figure 7.6).

2. *The Student's Current IEP Goals* should be included in the personal file to ensure that all of the student's teachers are aware of the student's targeted areas of need and modifications that are required to optimize student performance.

3. *The Snapshot Learner Form* provides the reader with a quick insight into the student with AS. This form assists teachers to develop educational programs centered on the specific needs of the student (see Chapter 2, Figure 2.1).

Figure 7.6   Personal File Inventory

Student Name
- Current IEP goals
- Snapshot Learner Form
- Reinforcement Checklist
- Student Interests Form
- Child Behavior Profile
- Daily Transition Checklist
- Strategy Form
- Teacher Notes
- Other information

4. *The Child Behavioral Profile* gives teachers a reference point to discuss concerns beyond academics, such as social/emotional issues, speech/language/hearing, vision, and motor concerns. This form can serve as an easy-to-complete screening device (see Figure 7.7).

5. *The Daily Transition Checklist* is a list of basic supports that provide the structure needed to ensure the success of daily transitions (see Table 7.4).

6. *The Strategies Form* allows teachers to see which strategies have been tried and their degree of success. The form may include a list of strategies that have been tried such as priming, modeling, video modeling (Figure 7.8), their effectiveness, a list of the student's special interests (see Table 7.6), and any other information that would help ease the transition for the student and provide strategies for the teacher.

7. *The Teacher's Notes Form* provides ongoing documentation of the student's activities, successes, and difficulties throughout the school day. The form Includes a brief summary statement (two to three sentences) and suggested follow-up needs (see Figure 7.9).

PLANNING FOR TRANSITION SERVICES

As part of the IEP process for students beginning in the eighth grade or at age 14, whichever comes first, IDEA requires that transition services be considered for the student. Development of a transition plan becomes part of the IEP process. Transition plans help guide students' course of study as they progress through high school and include a variety of activities and supports that provide opportunities to sample what is available after

Figure 7.7   Child Behavior Profile

Child Behavioral Profile

Directions: Please complete the following demographic information:

Child's Name _____   Birthdate _____

Age _____   Sex _____   Grade _____   Classroom Placement _____

Directions: Please check the behaviors that appear consistently in this child. To determine
whether or not the behavior(s) occur consistently, compare the child to peers.

Affective

____ withdrawn	____ consistent hunger
____ self-destructive behavior	____ avoids good touches
____ wary of adult contact	____ poor hygiene
____ demanding/clinging behavior	____ anger/hitting
____ sexual behavior/masturbation	____ sudden changes in behavior
____ unexplained welts/bruises	____ afraid to go home
____ reports of bedwetting	____ reports of nightmares
____ tells or draws violent stories	____ frequent complaints of illness

Vision

____ bloodshot, swollen, or teary eyes	____ facial twitching
____ blurred or double vision	____ itching/burning eyes
____ squints	____ rubs eyes
____ closes one eye while reading	____ holds head to one side when reading
____ holds books very near or far from eyes	____ strained or tense facial expression
____ alternately moves books towards or	____ confuses similar looking letters
away from eyes	(a/e, r/n)

Speech/Language/Hearing

____ indistinct/garbed speech	
____ confuses words of similar sounds	____ cups hand behind ears
____ voice to loud or soft	____ voice excessively nasal/hoarse
____ shows intense effort when listening	____ daydreaming/inattentiveness
____ frequent earaches, congestion, allergies	____ gestures instead of using words
____ facial grimacing when speaking	____ speaks to fast or slow
____ looks to peers before following teacher	____ word or phrase repetitions
instruction	____ refers to objects as things, those things
____ does not respond to speaker if he/she	____ usage of nonstandard letters
asks to have statement repeated	in words

From *Asperger Syndrome and Assessment Practical Solutions for Indentifying Students' Needs* by B. S. Myles, D. Andreon, and J. Stella (2005). Reprinted with permission from Autism Asperger Publishing Company, Shawnee Mission, KS.

high school. The student must be involved in this transition planning, identifying areas of interest and preferences. Transition plans must be revisited annually. The IEP team should ensure that courses being taken match anticipated activities after high school. Figures 7.10 and 7.11 provide planning documents that an IEP team might utilize while working

Figure 7.8   Strategy Form

Student: Geir Andre		Date: April 5
Strategy	Environment	Effectiveness
Visual schedule	❑ General Ed ❑ Special Ed ❑ Transitions • Community • Home • Other	❑ Works well ❑ Works with modification • Requires support • Requires redirection • Ineffective
Comments: The mini visual support seems to work well in all environments except PE. Visual supports help Geir Andre with following directions.		
Strategy	Environment	Effectiveness
Map of route from afternoon classes to his locker and back.	❑ General Ed • Special Ed ❑ Transitions • Community • Home • Other	❑ Works well • Works with modification • Requires support • Requires redirection • Ineffective
Comments: This is an amazing strategy that has worked wonders. Geir Andre is able to be completely independent during transitions in the afternoon.		
Strategy	Environment	Effectiveness
Peer note taking	❑ General Ed • Special Ed • Transitions • Community • Home • Other	• Works well • Works with modification • Requires support • Requires redirection ❑ Ineffective
Comments: This is a good idea but it did not work for Geir. The notes did not make sense to him and it only increased his frustration level.		

with a student with AS to develop a transition plan. Options available after high school can be divided into the following categories: postsecondary education, integrated employment (supported and independent employment), vocational training, adult services, independent living, and community participation, all of which are described below.

Postsecondary Education

Postsecondary education includes enrollment in a trade school, college, or university. To prepare for this type of environment, the student will need to focus on academic classes that give him or her the skills required for

Table 7.6   Student Interests Form

Location	Interest	Level of Support
Home	❑ Video games (especially car racing and basketball) Teddy enjoys playing video games but has difficulty changing activities. Setting a timer tells him when it is time to stop playing and do something else.	❑ Independent ❑ Shared (with): ❑ Supports needed ✓ timer
School	❑ Computer Although Teddy would rather work by himself, it is important for social skill building to work collaboratively. This group works well together with support. It helps all 3 students to have the visual choices. The timer assists with turn taking.	❑ Independent ❑ Shared (with): Alethea and Annie ❑ Supports needed: ✓ timer ✓ specific visual game choices
Other	❑ Scouts Teddy likes earning and collecting badges. Because he is, at times, rigid, his environment must be structured and predictable. Having a visual agenda for him will ease his anxiety. A visual schedule will allow him to participate in the activities with minimal adult direction. It is important for staff to allow at least 10 seconds processing time before expecting an answer to any question. Using small hand fidgets (such as a small squish ball, stretchy snake, pencil grip, etc.) will help keep him focused. REMEMBER just because he is not looking at you does not mean he is not paying attention.	❑ Independent ❑ Shared (with): Scout troop (9 boys and 2 leaders) ❑ Supports needed: ✓ visual meeting agenda, visual schedule strips for specific activities ✓ assigned seat for table activities ✓ extra processing time for answers to questions ✓ hand fidgets for calming

success on state standardized achievement instruments, learn independent study skills, decide on an area of focus (major), learn skills to advocate for accommodations and services (academic, social, and behavioral) to help him or her succeed, and learn age-appropriate social and self-help skills. Figure 7.12 outlines tasks that a student might complete annually for a successful transition from high school to the adult world.

Trey, an eighth grader with AS, has above-average intelligence and is gifted in the areas of math and science. Trey enjoys figuring out scientific equations in his free time and taking part in Math and Science Clubs.

Figure 7.9   Teacher Notes Form

Dates/Events	Summary	Follow-Up
October 23	Tried having Jamal sit near the front of the room on the outside row today. He was able to stay focused and he participated in the reading discussion.	
October 29	Great time in library. It helped that the topic was about dinosaurs, one of his special interests.	
November 16	Rough day for Jamal. Refused to do any writing. Threw his pencil on the floor several times.	Check with OT for suggestions.
December 1	Jamal is learning to keyboard, and in the meantime is dictating writing assignments to me. Inappropriate behaviors have increased.	

During school, Trey socializes very little with other students. Often during class he will make fun of students who are unable to grasp the basic math and science concepts that he finds easy. Trey's peers find him to be mean spirited and do not like to be partnered with him. During classes when being partnered is required, students voice their dislike of Trey. Trey does not understand why the other students don't like him and acts out by loudly telling people they are stupid and dumb during class and is getting into fights in the hallway in between classes.

Academically he does very well, but it appears that he needs assistance with his social skills. His IEP team, in consultation with the guidance department, decided that Trey would benefit from taking advanced placement (AP) classes in math and science during his freshman and sophomore years and college classes in those subjects during his junior and senior years. At the end of Trey's sophomore year the team anticipates that he will begin looking at universities, decide on an area of study, and during the fall of his junior year he may begin the college application process. His transition plan reflects this information.

Academically, Trey seems to fit the postsecondary education track. To address Trey's social skill deficits, the IEP team decided that he would benefit from attending a social skills class offered by the school. He has specific social skills that he must improve (i.e., not making fun of his peers, not fighting in the hallway) over the four years of high school. The IEP team, considering his transition planning, made sure that all of Trey's teachers were aware of his social skills goals each week, and that data was collected on his progress. Each week that goals are met, Trey works a new problem with the physics teacher. In planning for his future, the team has considered his needs and interests and communicated them to the staff that work with him. The team will reassess this path at least annually, at his IEP meeting.

(Text continues on page 155)

Figure 7.10 High School Graduation Planning Document

Credit Requirements:	9th	10th	11th	12th	13th	14th	15th
English							
Mathematics							
History/Social Sciences							
Science							
Foreign Language							
Health & PE							
Fine/Practical Arts							
Electives							
Total							

High School Graduation Planner: 4, 5, 6, or 7 Year Plan for Students With IEPs

Career Interest Area:

Diploma Choice:

Fairfax County Public Schools, Department of Special Services, Office of Special Education, Career and Transition Services Section. Used with permission.

Figure 7.11 Transition Planning Worksheet

Where do you want to be at age 25?	Post-Secondary Requirements	High School Requirements	Middle School Requirements
Career Goal:	Education: Training: Testing: Experience:	Diploma: Courses: Testing: Experience:	Benchmarks: Courses: Experience:
Personal Goal:	Skills Training: Experience:	Skills Training: Experience:	Skills Training: Experience:

What are possible barriers to reaching my goals?

What steps will I take this year to help me reach my goals?

Fairfax County Public Schools, Department of Special Services, Office of Special Education, Career and Transition Services Section. Used with permission.

Figure 7.12 Transition Timeline

Middle School Tasks

☐ Develop study skills and strategies that you know work for you

☐ Talk to teachers to identify classroom accommodation needs

☐ Evaluate basic skills in reading, mathematics, oral and written language, and plan for remediation if necessary

☐ Identify tentative post-secondary career and personal goals

☐ Investigate which high school classes will best prepare you for your post-secondary goals

☐ Attend high school orientation or schedule appointment with high school special education department chair to familiarize yourself with high school requirements

☐ Review high school diploma options and plan course of study to meet requirements

☐ Explore interests through elective courses, clubs, and/or extracurricular activities

☐ Investigate 9th grade vocational class to see if it offers training relevant to your post-secondary goals

☐ Begin a Transition Services Career Portfolio to collect information that may be helpful in planning for your future

☐ Review high school diploma options and plan course of study to meet requirements

☐ Take the state required standardized tests in English and Mathematics at the end of eighth grade

☐ Participate in developing a transition plan, which will be included in your IEP starting in 8th grade (or at age 14)

☐ Attend IEP meeting

☐ Make a list of the activities necessary to achieve your transition plan goals

Freshman Year Tasks

☐ Learn the specific nature of your disability and how to explain it so others will understand your needs

☐ Ask your parent or a special education teacher to help you develop a plan for meeting with your teachers to explain your disability and request accommodations

☐ Learn strategies to help you access the same course work as your peers

☐ Continue to remediate basic skill deficits

☐ Review diploma options, revise choice as necessary, and plan course of study to meet requirements

☐ Consider whether extending your high school graduation date by one to three years will help you to reach your post-secondary goals

☐ Discuss with guidance counselor appropriateness of enrollment in 10th grade career-related courses

☐ Visit the school career center and ask the Career Center Specialist to tell you about the college and career planning resources available in your school

☐ Meet with your case manager to discuss the comprehensive vocational assessment services offered locally to decide whether a referral is appropriate

☐ Continue to explore interests through elective courses, clubs, and extracurricular activities

☐ Update your Career Portfolio

Figure 7.12

☐ Meet with your case manager to plan your IEP meeting and to discuss the role you will play in development of your IEP

☐ Formulate a transition plan with your case manager and IEP team that reflects your goals and interests

☐ Prepare for and pass the required standardized tests

Sophomore Year Tasks

☐ Ask your parent or special education teacher to help you prepare to meet with your teachers to explain your disability and request accommodations.

☐ Add to your understanding and use of learning strategies to help you access the same course work as your peers

☐ Continue to remediate basic skill deficits

☐ Review diploma options, revise choice as necessary, and plan course of study to meet requirements

☐ Consider whether extending your high school graduation date by one to three years will help you to reach your post-secondary goals

☐ Discuss with guidance counselor appropriateness of enrollment in career-related courses

☐ Meet with your case manager to discuss available career/vocational assessment options to decide whether a referral is appropriate

☐ If your career plans will require a college degree, register and take the Preliminary Scholastic Aptitude Test (PSAT) in the fall — consider using testing adjustments and auxiliary aids

☐ Continue to explore interests through extracurricular activities, hobbies, volunteer work, and work experiences

☐ Identify interests, aptitudes, values, and opportunities related to occupations in which you are interested

☐ Update your Career Portfolio

☐ Participate actively in your IEP meeting

☐ Continue to actively participate in your IEP transition planning with your case manager and IEP team

Junior Year Tasks

☐ Identify the appropriate academic adjustments and auxiliary aids and services that you will need in the postsecondary setting and learn how to use them efficiently

☐ Learn time management, study skills, assertiveness training, stress management, and exam preparation strategies

☐ Arrange to meet with your teachers to explain your disability and request accommodations

☐ Continue to remediate basic skill deficits

☐ Review diploma options, revise choice as necessary, and plan course of study to meet requirements

☐ Consider whether extending your high school graduation date by one to three years will help you to reach your post-secondary goals.

☐ Discuss with guidance counselor appropriateness of enrollment in 12th grade in career-related courses

(Continued)

Figure 7.12

☐ Meet with your case manager to discuss available career/vocational assessment options to decide whether a referral is appropriate

☐ Continue to explore your interests through involvement in school- or community-based extracurricular activities and work experiences

☐ Update your Career Portfolio

☐ Focus on matching your interests and abilities to the appropriate post-secondary goals

☐ If your career goals require post-secondary education, look for schools that have courses in which you might be interested

☐ Speak with representatives of colleges, technical schools, training programs, and/or the military who visit your high school or present at college and postsecondary fairs

☐ Gather information about college programs that offer the disability services you need

☐ Visit campuses and their disability service offices to verify the available services and how to access them

☐ Make sure that the documentation of your disability is current. Colleges want current evaluations, usually less than three years old when you begin college

☐ Ask your guidance counselor about the differences between SAT and ACT tests to determine which better matches your learning style

☐ Consider taking a course to prepare for the SAT or for the ACT

☐ Take the SAT or ACT in the spring. Discuss with your case manager whether to request testing accommodations

☐ Meet with your case manager to develop a plan for leading your IEP

☐ Continue to participate in your IEP transition planning with your case manager and IEP team

☐ Contact the Department of Rehabilitative Services (DRS), the Community Services Board, or other post-secondary agencies to determine your eligibility for services

☐ Invite a representative of the appropriate adult services agency to attend your IEP meeting

Senior (or 18-22) Year Tasks

☐ Identify ways in which the accommodations listed on your IEP will translate to post-secondary education and employment settings

☐ Continue to develop your advocacy skills and to polish study skills

☐ Arrange to meet with your teachers to explain your disability and request accommodations.

☐ Continue to remediate basic skill deficits

☐ Review diploma options, revise choice as necessary, and plan course of study to meet requirements.

☐ Consider whether extending your high school graduation date by one to three years will help you to reach your post-secondary goals.

☐ Discuss with guidance counselor appropriateness of enrollment during 5th, 6th or 7th year of high school in career-related courses

☐ Meet with your case manager to discuss available career/vocational assessment options to decide whether a referral is appropriate

☐ Continue to explore your interests through involvement in school- or community-based extracurricular activities and work experiences

☐ Update your Career Portfolio

☐ Focus on matching your interests and abilities to the appropriate post-secondary goals

(Continued)

Figure 7.12 (Continued)

☐ Meet with your school guidance counselor early in the year to discuss your postsecondary plans.

☐ Plan to visit schools, colleges, or training programs in which you are interested early in the year

☐ Evaluate the disability services, service provider, and staff of any schools in which you are interested

☐ Obtain copies of any school records that document your disability in order to obtain accommodations in post-secondary environments

☐ Take the SAT or ACT again, if appropriate

☐ Lead your IEP meeting

☐ Develop your Individual Transition Plan and present it at your IEP meeting

☐ If not done in your junior year, contact the Department of Rehabilitative Services (DRS), the Community Services Board, or other adult service agency counselor to determine your eligibility for post-secondary services

☐ Invite a representative of the appropriate adult services agency to attend your IEP meeting

---

Fairfax County Public Schools, Department of Special Services, Office of Special Education, Career and Transition Services Section. Used with permission.

Integrated Employment

Integrated employment is an option available to any individual and can be accessed during high school as well as beyond. Many schools offer supported vocational courses that allow students to master required prerequisite job skills and then practice them in a supported environment. The IEP team needs to look closely at the individual's needs and interests when planning for employment. They must also consider the type of social or academic skills the student needs, and accommodations and supports that may be required for the student to complete the job independently. Once these items are assessed, the IEP team can determine whether the student benefits from independent employment or vocational services.

In *independent employment,* the individual works and receives all of his or her training from the employer. For individuals who need continual training and assistance, *vocational* programs offer a variety of services such as *work training* (work adjustments), *supported employment,* and *facility-based employment* (sheltered workshop). Murray, a tenth grader with AS, has average intelligence. He enjoys working with his hands and appears gifted mechanically. Murray experiences challenges in larger group with less structured situations due to the noise and confusion common to those situations. He reacts with verbal outbursts, pacing behaviors, and at times aggressive behaviors that make it difficult for him with peers. Murray's IEP team decided when he was 14 that a work training or supported employment program might suit him. His parents had toured three different vocational programs with him. Working in conjunction with his IEP team, a program was devised for Murray. He spends part of his day in a smaller group academic setting, and part of his day learning skills in a vocational supported employment setting. The IEP team considered Murray's strengths and interest when considering transition options for him.

Persons taking part in *work training* or *work adjustments* attend a vocational training center for a specific period of time to sample a variety of jobs, receive training, and then receive assistance in finding a permanent job in the community. This is typically arranged through the Department of Vocational Rehabilitation. Persons in *supported employment* have paid employment in the community as part of work crews or sometimes have individually tailored jobs. They receive consistent on-the-job training, assistance in finding an appropriate job, and follow-up with the employer to make sure they are following through on their job. *Facility-based employment* or *sheltered workshops* often provide a variety of work opportunities in a secure setting. Types of work may include shredding paper, packaging and assembly, recycling, custodial, and clerical work.

Adult Services

Eligibility for adult services must be documented based on disability. After a student leaves high school, she is no longer entitled to receive special education services. As described in Figure 7.4, beginning at age 16 a statement of needed transition services, including a statement of interagency responsibilities, must be included in the IEP. It is very important that the IEP team determines services necessary after graduation. Two important service providers are Social Security Administration (SSA) and Vocational Rehabilitation System (VRS). SSA provides individuals with cash and health benefits, and VRS can provide job training and placement. Other services are available based on disability, so it is important to investigate each service, determine eligibility as it relates to each individual, and determine services available for the future.

Independent Living

Independent living is part of most adults' lives. Unfortunately, in many states there are more needs than services, so being proactive in anticipating the individual's need is important. Available living situations include:

1. Independent living options, which are just that, independent. Individuals are responsible for all aspects of taking care of themselves and their home.

2. Semi-independent living options, which often consist of apartment units with available staff.

3. Group homes, which have staff that provide care, training, and supervision.

4. Residential care facilities, which provide around-the-clock supervision, training, and more extensive care and support than what is received in a group home or semi-independent living.

Community Participation

Community participation is an important part of being an adult. Persons with AS generally have difficulty with socialization, so it is very important that supports are put in place to assist the individual with being an active participant in his or her community by taking part in leisure and social activities.

When planning transition services, it is extremely important to incorporate a team approach. This team should include not only school personnel, parents, and the student but also local agencies such as Department of Vocational Rehabilitation, vocational services, and independent or supported living centers.

SUMMARY

When considering any type of transition for a student with AS, it is important to provide predictability in his or her day, environment, academic activities, and social routines. Effective transition planning reduces the stress and anxiety that change brings to students with AS while allowing them opportunities to be successful. Transitions take time, commitment, and an understanding of the student's strengths and challenges. Remember to PLAN (see Table 7.7).

Table 7.7	PLAN	
P	Proactive	Plan ahead for success.
L	Look/Listen	Observe student's stress and anxiety level.
A	Assess	Check progress regularly.
N	Navigate	Make modifications and accommodations as needed.

References

Albert, L. (1989). *A teacher's guide to cooperative discipline: How to manage your classroom and promote self-esteem.* Circle Pines, MN: American Guidance Service.

American Psychiatric Association. (1994). *Diagnostic and statistical manual of mental disorders* (4th ed.). Washington, DC: Author.

American Psychiatric Association. (2000). *Diagnostic and statistical manual of mental disorders* (4th ed., text revision). Washington, DC: Author.

Arwood, E., & Brown, M. M. (1999). *A guide to cartooning and flowcharting: See the ideas.* Portland, OR: Apricot.

Asperger, H. (1944). Die 'Autistischen Psychopathen' im Kindesalter ["Autistic Psychopathy" in Childhood]. *Archiv fur Psychiatrie und Nervenkrankheiten, 117,* 76–136.

Ayres, A. J. (1979). *Sensory integration and the child.* Los Angeles: Western Psychological Services.

Backes, C. E., & Ellis, I. C. (2003). The secret of classroom management. *Techniques, 78*(5), 22–25.

Baker, J. E. (2003). *Social skills training for children and adolescents with Asperger Syndrome and social communication problems.* Shawnee Mission, KS: Autism Asperger Publishing Company.

Barnhill, G. P. (2001). Social attribution and depression in adolescents with Asperger Syndrome. *Focus on Autism and Other Developmental Disabilities, 16,* 46–53.

Barnhill, G., Hagiwara, T., Myles, B. S., & Simpson, R. L. (2000). Asperger Syndrome: A study of the cognitive profiles of 37 children and adolescents. *Focus on Autism and Other Developmental Disabilities, 15,* 146–153.

Barnhill, G. P., Hagiwara, T., Myles, B. S., Simpson, R. L., Brick, M. L., & Griswold, D. E. (2000). Parent, teacher, and self-report of problem and adaptive behaviors in children and adolescents with Asperger Syndrome. *Diagnostique, 25,* 147–167.

Baron-Cohen, S., O'Riordan, M., Stone, V., Jones, R., & Plaisted, K. (1999). Recognition of faux pas by normally developing children and children with Asperger Syndrome or high-functioning autism. *Journal of Autism and Developmental Disorders, 29,* 407–418.

Beck, M. (1987). Understanding and managing the acting-out child. *The Pointer, 29*(2), 27–29.

Bieber, J. (Producer). (1994). *Learning disabilities and social skills with Richard LaVoie: Last one picked . . . first one picked on* [Television broadcast]. Washington, DC: Public Broadcasting Service.

Broderick, C., Caswell, R., Gregor, S., Marzolini, S., & Wilson, O. (2002). 'Can I join the club?': A social integration scheme for adolescents with Asperger Syndrome. *Autism: The International Journal of Research and Practice, 6*, 427–432.

Bromley, K., Irwin-DeVitis, L., & Modio, M. (1995). *Graphic organizers: Visual strategies for active learning.* New York: Scholastic.

Bryant, D. P., & Bryant, B. R. (2004). *Assistive technology for people with disabilities.* Boston, MA: Allyn & Bacon.

Buggey, R. (1999). Videotaped self-modeling: Allowing children to be their own models. *Teaching Exceptional Children, 4*, 27–31.

Buggey, T., Toombs, K., Gardener, P., & Cervetti, M. (1999). Training responding behaviors in students with autism: Using videotaped self-modeling. *Journal of Positive Behavioral Interventions, 1*, 205–214.

Buron, K. D. (2003). *When my autism gets too big! A relaxation book for children with autism spectrum disorders.* Shawnee Mission, KS: Autism Asperger Publishing Company.

Buron, K. D., & Curtis, M. (2003). *The incredible 5-point scale.* Shawnee Mission, KS: Autism Asperger Publishing Company.

Charlop-Christy, M. H., & Daneshvar, S. (2003). Using video modeling to teach perspective taking to children with autism. *Journal of Positive Behavior Interventions, 5*, 12–21.

Charlop-Christy, M. H., Le, L., & Freeman, K. A. (2000). A comparison of video modeling with in-vivo modeling for teaching children with autism. *Journal of Autism and Developmental Disorders, 30*, 537–552.

Church, C., Alisanski, S., & Amanullah, S. (2000). The social behavioral and academic experiences of children with Asperger Syndrome. *Focus on Autism and Other Developmental Disabilities, 15*, 12–20.

Cognition and Technology Group at Vanderbilt. (1993). The Jasper experiment: An exploration of issues in learning and instruction design. *Educational Technology Research and Development, 40*, 65–80.

Davies, D., Stock, S. E., & Wehmeyer, M. (2002). Enhancing independent task performance for individuals with mental retardation through use of a handheld self-directed visual and audio prompting system. *Education and Training in Mental Retardation and Developmental Disabilities, 37*(2), 209–218.

Dowrick, P. W. (1999). A review of self modeling and related interventions. *Applied and Preventive Psychology, 8*, 23–29.

Dowrick, P. W., & Dove, C. (1980). The use of self-modeling to improve the swimming performance of spina bifida children. *Journal of Applied Behavior Analysis, 13*, 51–56.

Dowrick, P. W., & Raeburn, J. M. (1995). Self-modeling: Rapid skills training for children with physical disabilities. *Journal of Developmental and Physical Disabilities, 7*, 25–37.

Dunn, W., Myles, B. S., & Orr, S. (2002). Sensory processing issues associated with Asperger Syndrome: A preliminary investigation. *The American Journal of Occupational Therapy, 56*(1), 97–102.

Durand & Crimmins (1992). *Motivation assessment scale.* Topeka, KS: Monaco & Associates.

Edyburn, D. (2000). Assistive technology and students with mild disabilities. *Focus on Exceptional Children, 32*(9), 1–24.

Ehlers, S., & Gillberg, C. (1993). The epidemiology of Asperger Syndrome: A total population study. *Journal of Child Psychology and Psychiatry, 34,* 1237–1350.

Engstrom, I., Ekstrom, L., & Emilsson, B. (2003). Psychosocial functioning in a group of Swedish adults with Asperger Syndrome or high-functioning autism. *Autism: The International Journal of Research and Practice, 7,* 99–110.

Faherty, C. (2000). *What does it mean to me? A workbook explaining self-awareness and life lessons to the child or youth with high functioning autism or Asperger's.* Arlington, TX: Future Horizons.

Ferguson, H., Myles, B. S., & Hagiwara, T. (in press). Using a personal digital assistant to enhance the independence of an adolescent with Asperger Syndrome. *Education and Training in Developmental Disabilities.*

Frith, U. (Ed.). (1991). *Autism and Asperger Syndrome.* Cambridge, UK: Cambridge University Press.

Furick, P. K. (2003). Teaching mind-reading: Making sense of behavior. *Closing The Gap, 22*(3), 1.

Gagnon, E. (2001). *The Power Card strategy: Using special interests to motivate children and youth with Asperger Syndrome and autism.* Shawnee Mission, KS: Autism Asperger Publishing Company.

Gagnon, E., & Myles, B. S. (1999). *This is Asperger Syndrome.* Shawnee Mission, KS: Autism Asperger Publishing Company.

Ghaziuddin, M., Weidmar-Mikhail, E., & Ghaziuddin, N. (1998). Comorbidity of Asperger Syndrome: A preliminary report. *Autism, 42,* 279–283.

Gill, V. (2003). Challenges faced by teachers working with students with Asperger Syndrome. In M. Prior (Ed.), *Learning and behavior problems in Asperger Syndrome* (pp. 194–211). New York: Guilford Press.

Gray, C. (1995). *Social stories unlimited: Social stories and comic strip conversations.* Jenison, MI: Jenison Public Schools.

Gray, C. (2000). *Writing social stories with Carol Gray.* Arlington, TX: Future Horizons.

Gray, C. A., & Gerand, J. D. (1993). Social stories: Improving responses of students with autism with accurate social information. *Focus on Autistic Behavior, 8,* 1–10.

Green, R. W. (1998). *The explosive child: A new approach to understanding and parenting easily frustrated "chronically inflexible" children.* New York: HarperCollins.

Griswold, D. E., Barnhill, G. P., Myles, B. S., Hagiwara, T., & Simpson, R. L. (2002). Asperger Syndrome and academic achievement. *Focus on Autism and Other Developmental Disabilities, 17,* 94–102.

Gutstein, S. E., & Sheely, R. K. (2002). *Relationship development intervention with children and adolescents and adults: Social and emotional development activities for Asperger Syndrome, autism, PDD, and NLD.* London: Jessica Kingsley.

Henry Occupational Therapy Services, Inc. (1998). *Tool chest: For teachers, parents, and students.* Youngstown, AZ: Author.

Hersh, R. H., & Walker, H. M. (1983). Great expectations: making schools effective for all students. *Policy Studies Review, 2,* 147–188.

Howlin, P., Baron-Coehn, S., & Hadwin, J. (1999). *Teaching children with autism to mind-read: A practical guide for teachers and parents.* New York: John Wiley and Sons.

Ives, M. (2001). *What is Asperger Syndrome, and how will it affect me? A guide for young people.* Shawnee Mission, KS: Autism Asperger Publishing Company.

Jones, T., Myles, B. S., Gagnon, E., & Hagiwara, H. (2004). *Using a personal digital assistant to assist a student with Asperger Syndrome in controlling inappropriate verbalizations.* Manuscript in preparation.

Kadesjo, B., Gillberg, C., & Hagberg, B. (1999). Autism and Asperger Syndrome in seven-year-old children: A total population study. *Journal of Autism and Developmental Disorders, 29,* 327–332.

Kahn, J. S., Kehle, T. J., Jenson, W. R., & Clark, E. (1990). Comparison of cognitive-behavioral relaxation, and self-modeling interventions for depression among middle-school students. *School Psychology Review, 19,* 196–211.

Kamps, D. M., Kravits, T., & Ross, M. (2002). Social-communicative strategies for school-age children. In H. Goldstein, L. A. Kaczmarek, & K. M. English (Eds.), *Promoting social communication: Children with developmental disabilities from birth to adolescence* (pp. 239–277). Baltimore, MD: Paul H. Brookes.

Kern, Dunlap, Clarke & Childs (1994). *Student-assisted functional-assessment interview form.*

Kerr, M. M., & Zigmond, N. (1986). What do high school teachers want? A study of expectations and standards. *Education and Treatment of Children, 9,* 239–249.

Kim, J. A., Szatmari, P., Bryson, S. E., Streiner, D. L., & Wilson, F. J. (2000). The prevalence of anxiety and mood problems among children with autism and Asperger Syndrome. *Autism, 4,* 117–32.

Klin, A., & Volkmar, F. R. (2000). Treatment and intervention guidelines for individuals with Asperger Syndrome. In A. Klin, F. R. Volkmar, & S. S. Sparrow (Eds.), *Asperger Syndrome* (pp. 340–366). New York: Guilford Press.

Klin, A., Volkmar, F., & Sparrow, S. S. (2000). *Asperger Syndrome.* New York: Guilford Press.

Koning, C., & McGill-Evans, J. (2001). Social and language skills in adolescent boys with Asperger Syndrome. *Autism: The International Journal of Research and Practice, 5,* 23–36.

Kransy, L., Williams, B. J., Provencal, S., & Ozonoff, S. (2003). Social skills interventions for the autism spectrum: Essential ingredients and a model curriculum. *Child and Adolescent Psychiatric Clinic of North America, 12,* 107–122.

Lane, K. L., Pierson, M. R., & Givner, C. C. (2003). Teacher expectations of student behavior: Which skills do elementary and secondary teachers deem necessary for success in the classroom? *Education and Treatment of Children, 26,* 413–418.

Ledgin, N. (2002). *Asperger's and self-esteem: Insight and hope through famous role models.* Arlington, TX: Future Horizons.

Lenz, B. K., Bulgren, J. A., Schumaker, J. B., Deshler, D. D., & Boudah, D. J. (1994). *The unit organizer routine.* Lawrence, KS: Edge Enterprises.

Lewis, Scott, & Sungai (1994). *Problem behavior questionnaire:* A teacher-based instrument to develop functional hypothesis of problem behavior in general education classrooms. *Diagnostique.*

Long, N. J., Morse, W. C., & Newman, R. G. (1976). *Conflict in the classroom: Educating children with problems* (3rd ed.). Belmont, CA: Wadsworth.

Marks, S. U., Shaw-Hegwer, J., Schrader, C., Longaker, T., Peters, I., Powers, F., et al. (2003). Instructional management tips for teachers of students with autism spectrum disorder. *Teaching Exceptional Children, 34,* 50–55.

Martin, J. (2002). Transition: The foundation of secondary educational programs. *Beyond Behavior, 12,* 27–28.

McAfee, J. (2002). *Navigating the social world: A curriculum for individuals with Asperger's Syndrome, high functioning autism, and related disorders.* Arlington, TX: Future Horizons.

Moore, S. T. (2002). *Asperger Syndrome and the elementary school experience: Practical solutions for academic and social difficulties.* Shawnee Mission, KS: Autism Asperger Publishing Company.

Morgenstern, J., & Morgenstern-Colón, J. (2002). *Organizing from the inside out for teens: The foolproof system for organizing your room, your time, and your life.* New York: Henry Holt.

Moyes, R. A. (2001). *Incorporating social goals in the classroom.* London: Jessica Kingsley.

Myles, B. S., & Adreon, D. (2001). *Asperger Syndrome and adolescence: Practical solutions for school success.* Shawnee Mission, KS: Autism Asperger Publishing Company.

Myles, B. S., Bock, S. J., & Simpson, R. L. (2000). *The Asperger Syndrome Diagnostic Scale.* Austin, TX: Pro-Ed.

Myles, B. S., Cook, K. T., Miller, N. E., Rinner, L., & Robbins, L. (2000). *Asperger Syndrome and sensory issues: Practical solutions for making sense of the world.* Shawnee Mission, KS: Autism Asperger Publishing Company.

Myles, B. S., Ferguson, H., & Hagiwara, T. (in press). Using a personal digital assistant to improve homework recording by an adolescent with Asperger Syndrome. *Journal of Special Education Technology.*

Myles, B. S., Hagiwara, R., Dunn, W., Rinner, L., Reese, M., Huggins, A., et al. (2004). Sensory issues in children with Asperger Syndrome and autism. *Education and Training in Developmental Disabilities, 39,* 283–290.

Myles, B. S., Huggins, A., Rome-Lake, M., Hagiwara, R., Barnhill, G. P., & Griswold, D. E. (2003). Written language profile of children and youth with Asperger Syndrome. *Education and Training in Developmental Disabilities, 38,* 362–370.

Myles, B. S., Keeling, K., & Van Horn, C. (2001). Studies using the Power Card strategy. In E. Gagnon (Ed.), *The Power Card strategy: Using special interests to motivate children and youth with Asperger Syndrome and autism* (pp. 51–57). Shawnee Mission, KS: Autism Asperger Publishing Company.

Myles, B. S., & Simpson, R. L. (2001). Understanding the hidden curriculum: An essential social skill for children and youth with Asperger Syndrome. *Intervention in School and Clinic, 36,* 279–286.

Myles, B. S., & Simpson, R. L. (2002). Students with Asperger Syndrome: Implications for counselors. *Counseling and Human Development, 34*(7), 1–14.

Myles, B. S., & Simpson, R. L. (2003). *Asperger Syndrome: A guide for educators and parents* (2nd ed.). Austin, TX: Pro-Ed.

Myles, B. S., & Southwick, J. (1999). *Asperger Syndrome and difficult moments: Practical solutions for tantrums, rage, and meltdowns.* Shawnee Mission, KS: Autism Asperger Publishing Company.

Myles, B. S., Trautman, M., & Schelvan, R. (2004). *Asperger Syndrome and the hidden curriculum: Practical solutions for understanding unwritten rules.* Shawnee Mission, KS: Autism Asperger Publishing Company.

Ottinger, B. (2003). *Tictionary: A reference guide to the world of Tourette Syndrome, Asperger Syndrome, Attention Deficit Hyperactivity Disorder, and Obsessive Compulsive Disorder for parents and professionals.* Shawnee Mission, KS: Autism Asperger Publishing Company.

Packer, A. J. (1992). *Bringing up parents: The teenager's handbook.* Minneapolis, MN: Free Spirit.

Packer, A. J. (1997). *How rude: The teenagers' guide to good manners, proper behavior, and not grossing people out.* Minneapolis, MN: Free Spirit.

Phelan, P., Yu, H. C., & Davidson, A. L. (1994). Navigating the psychosocial pressures of adolescence: The voices and experiences of high school youth. *American Educational Research Journal, 31*, 415–447.

Prior, M. (2003). *Learning and behavior problems in Asperger Syndrome.* New York: Guilford Press.

Savner, J. L., & Myles, B. S. (2000). *Making visual supports work in the home and community for individuals with Asperger Syndrome and autism.* Shawnee Mission, KS: Autism Asperger Publishing Company.

Sweeney, C. (2003, November). *The CIRCUIT evaluation.* Presentation for the Topeka ARC, Topeka, KS.

Technology-Related Assistance with Disabilities Act of 1988, Pub. L. No. 100–407. Retrieved November 20, 2004, from www.ed.gov/pubs/Biennial/336.html.

Volkmar, F., & Klin, A. (2000). Diagnostic issues. In A. Klin, F. Volkmar, & S. Sparrow (Eds.), *Asperger Syndrome* (pp. 25–71). New York: Guilford Press.

Walker, H., & Rankin, R. (1983). Assessing the behavioral expectations and demands of less restrictive settings. *School Psychology Review, 12*, 274–284.

Wechsler, D. (1989). *Wechsler preschool and Primary Scale of Intelligence-Revised.* New York: Psychological Corporation.

Wechsler, D. (1991). *Wechsler Intelligence Scale for Children* (3rd ed.). New York: Psychological Corporation.

Williams, K. (2001). Understanding the student with Asperger Syndrome: Guidelines for teachers. *Intervention in School and Clinic, 36*, 287–292.

Wing, L. (1981). Asperger Syndrome: A clinical account. *Psychological Medicine, 11*, 115–129.

Yack, E., Sutton, S., & Aquilla, P. (1998). *Building bridges through sensory integration.* Weston, Ontario: Authors.

Index

**CORWIN
PRESS**

The Corwin Press logo—a raven striding across an open book—represents the union of courage and learning. Corwin Press is committed to improving education for all learners by publishing books and other professional development resources for those serving the field of K–12 education. By providing practical, hands-on materials, Corwin Press continues to carry out the promise of its motto: **"Helping Educators Do Their Work Better."**